Happy Birthday

"1980"

Loretta & Freddie

MiG PILOT

MiG PILOT
The Final Escape of Lieutenant Belenko

John Barron

READER'S DIGEST PRESS

McGRAW-HILL BOOK COMPANY

New York   St. Louis   San Francisco

Dusseldorf   London   Mexico   Sydney

3 4 5 6 7 8 9 D O D O 8 7 6 5 4 3 2 1 0

LIBRARY OF CONGRESS CATALOGING IN PUBLICATION DATA
Barron, John, 1930–
    MiG pilot.
    1. Belenko, Viktor.   2. Fighter pilots—
Russia—Biography.   3. Defectors—Russia—Biography.
4. MIG-25 (Jet fighter plane)   I. Title.
UG626.2.B44B37   1980   358.4'14'0924   [B]
ISBN 0-07-003850-3   79-20611

Book design Gloria Gentile

Editorial from the *Los Angeles Times*, copyright © 1976
Los Angeles Times. Reprinted by permission.

Contents

MiG PILOT

Into the Unknown

As he had done every day except Sunday during the past four weeks, Lieutenant Viktor Ivanovich Belenko awakened himself early to watch what the dawn might reveal. The first light was promising, and upon seeing the fiery, blinding sun rise, he knew: almost certainly this would be the day. Above the vast forests of pine, cedar, birch, and poplar stretching along the Pacific shores of the Soviet Far East, the sky was azure and cloudless. The magnificent weather meant that barring mistakes, malfunctions, or some other vagary, in all likelihood he would fly as scheduled. Probably he finally could attempt the supreme mission which rain, fuel shortages, or bureaucratic caprice repeatedly had forestalled. If the weather held, his chances of reaching the objective would be as good as he ever could expect.

Belenko estimated it all should be over within the next six hours. At age twenty-nine, he would be either dead or reborn into a new world. He felt tension in the muscles of the arms, legs, and stomach, but the stress derived more from the complexity of the mental tasks ahead than from fear of dying. During his training as a MiG (Named for its designers, Mikoyan and Gurevich) pilot he had lived on the edge of death so long and seen sudden, violent death so often that he had given up contemplating it. He had come to regard it simply as an unfathomable phenomenon to be avoided as long as possible, but not at any price. Neither did he dwell on the infinite uncertainties and unknowns that awaited him should he succeed and survive. He had assessed them as best he could before making his decision, and there was no profit in considering them further now. The awareness that he was looking for the last time at his pretty wife and three-year-old son, both sleeping within his reach near the window, evoked no emotion either. She had adamantly demanded a divorce and had announced her intent to take their child back to her parents in Magadan, some 1,250 miles away. The many failed attempts at reconciliation had sapped all emotion from the marriage, and there was nothing more to say. He was tempted to pick up and hold his son. *No! Don't! He might cry. You wouldn't ordinarily pick him up at this hour. Don't do one thing that you wouldn't ordinarily do.*

Belenko put on his shirt, trousers, and boots quickly, trying not to awaken his family or the family occupying the other room of the apartment. From between the pages of a tattered Russian-English dictionary he removed a slip of paper on which he had written a three-sentence message succinctly explaining his mission. Preparation of the message the month before and its retention ever since had been dangerous. Yet it was necessary that he deliver a written message instantly if all went well, so he folded the paper into a tight square and buried it in his pocket.

In the small yard outside the frame apartment house reserved for officers, he exercised for fifteen minutes, doing push-ups on soggy ground and chinning himself from the limb of a tree. Then he commenced jogging through the muddy streets of Chuguyevka, a village situated in the taiga 120 miles northeast of Vladivostok, toward the bus stop about a mile away. Running and jumping puddles, Belenko looked like a prototype of the New Communist Man the Party spoke endlessly of creating. He stood just over five feet eight inches and had an athletic physique, with broad, slightly sloping shoulders powerfully developed by years of boxing, arm wrestling, and calisthenics. A Soviet television program once pictured him—yellow hair, fair complexion, and large blue eyes widely set in a handsome, boyish face—as the very model of a young pilot. Women, particularly older women, were beguiled by his smile, which they found simultaneously shy and rakish.

At about seven that morning, September 6, 1976, Belenko arrived in a decrepit bus, built before World War II, at the headquarters compound of the 513th Fighter Regiment of the Soviet Air Defense Command. Outside the smallest of the red-and-white-brick buildings he hesitated. *No, you have to eat. You would be missed. Besides, you will need the strength. Go on!*

In the officers' mess, fresh white cloths covered the tables, each set for four pilots, and still-life paintings of fruit and vegetables adorned the walls. The waitresses, girls in the late teens or early twenties, all employed because they were pretty, enhanced the ambience. A physician was tasting the breakfast of goulash, rice, fruit compote, white bread, buttermilk, and tea to make sure it was fit for fliers. After he approved the food, everyone sat down in white plastic chairs and began.

Because Belenko was acting deputy commander of the 3rd Squadron, he customarily dined with the squadron commander, Yevgeny Petrovich Pankovsky. More often than not, by breakfast time Pankovsky's day had already started unhappily. The regimental commander, Lieutenant Colonel Yevgeny Ivanovich Shevsov, rose early to survey the wreckage visited upon his domain during the night, and by six-thirty he had the squadron commanders before him to berate and degrade them for the most recent transgressions of their underlings.

Shevsov was a sorely troubled officer. This was his first command, and the difficulties besetting the regiment would have taxed the capacities of the wisest and most experienced leader. He did not quite know how to cope, but he tried mightily, shouting, threatening, and often ridiculing officers in front of one another and the men. Other pilots dubbed him the Monster, but to Belenko he looked more like a toothless boxer dog: short, husky, with receding red hair, a protruding jaw, and a face that seemed in perpetual motion, as if he were chewing or growling.

Belenko greeted his squadron commander as always. "Good morning, Yevgeny Petrovich."

"You think it's a good morning? Do you know that already I got reamed? Did you know that our soldiers refused to eat breakfast this morning? They threw their food at the cooks, and one of them hit a cook."

"Would you eat that food from their mess hall?"

"No."

"I wouldn't eat that food either. I think if we would take a pig from a good *kolkhoz* and put that pig in the mess hall, that pig would faint."

"Well, I agree. But what can I do about it?"

At eight the regiment assembled on the asphalt parade ground before the staff headquarters buildings. Pilots stood at attention in the first rank; flight engineers, their assistants, and the enlisted men in succeeding ranks behind.

"Comrade Soldiers, Sergeants, and Officers!" Shevsov shouted. "Today we fly. Our mission is a vital mission, for we will fire rockets. The results of this important mission will depend on everybody, from soldiers to officers, working together. In spite of all our troubles here, we each must do our best today.

"We must remember that the Americans are not sleeping. We must remember that the Chinese are only a day's march away. We must remember that aircraft, fuel, and rockets are expensive and that our government which supplies them is not a milk cow. We cannot afford soon to repeat this mission, so we must do it properly today.

"Now, next weekend we will give the Party a Communist Weekend. Everybody will work, officers and soldiers; everybody. Each squadron must gather sod and plant it over the aircraft bunkers so that from the sky they will appear to the Americans to be no more than green, grassy fields.

"I have one other announcement, a very serious announcement. Do you know that our regiment has a great lover? Do you know whom he loves? Not his faithful wife who waits far away, anxious to join him here as soon as quarters are ready; no, he loves a whore in the village, a common whore." While the officers winced and the enlisted men snickered, Shevsov read aloud a telegram from the wife of a flight engineer, beseeching him to compel her husband to cease a dalliance of which she suspected him. "Here we have a big example of degenerate capitalist morality. Let this be a warning to all. Henceforth in our regiment we will abide by and tolerate only communist morality.

"All squadron commanders report to my office. For today that is all. Dismissed."

In the locker room Belenko changed into the dark-blue cotton flight suit issued him nineteen months before. It would be five more months before he was due to receive another, and he had tried to keep this one serviceable by neatly sewing patches on the knees and elbows. A duty officer unlocked the safe and handed him an automatic pistol and two clips of seven rounds each, for which he signed a receipt.

Sometime back a pilot had parachuted from a disabled plane into a remote wilderness, where he eventually died of privation and hunger. Hunters who came upon the skeleton many months later found a diary in which the pilot recorded his suffering and complained about the lack of any equipment that might have enabled him to survive in the wilderness. The last entry read, "Thank you, Party, for taking such good care of Soviet pilots." Soon combat pilots were issued pistols, and their aircraft equipped with survival kits containing food, water, medicine, fishing gear, flares, matches, a mirror, and shark repellent. Newly armed, a pilot came home, found his wife in bed with a friend, and killed them both. Thereupon, in the interest of domestic tranquillity, the Party ordered the pistols recalled and kept locked up until just before flights.

During the next couple of hours briefing officers meticulously reviewed the flight plans. Planes from the squadron designated to fire missiles were to fly almost due eastward over the sea, where Navy ships would launch the target drones at which they would shoot. Belenko's squadron would proceed to other exercise areas, practice intercept approaches, and then, relying solely on instruments, return to the base, and land. Because of the fine weather, many MiG-23s from adjacent bases probably would be in the air and perhaps also firing. Thus, it would be dangerous for any pilot to stray out of the zone to which Ground Control directed him.

Belenko sat motionless, maintaining a pose of respectful attentiveness while he contemplated his personal flight plan. His mind raced far away, computing times, distance, speed, fuel consumption, courses, points of probable intercept, evasive maneuvers, deceptions, and all exigencies he could imagine.

The fliers returned at eleven for a second breakfast of sausage, boiled eggs, white bread, butter, tea, and a chunk of chocolate, all again first tasted by a physician. Then a military truck hauled them over a bumpy, unpaved road to the Sakharovka Air Base two miles from squadron headquarters. Belenko presented himself in the hangar dispensary to the regimental physician for physical examination. The doctor protected the pilots as much as he could. They were forbidden to drink five days prior to flying; but everyone drank some, and many drank heavily. He ignored minor traces of alcohol, and if he judged the condition of a pilot hazardous in consequence of imbibing, he disqualified him for the day on other grounds—nasal congestion, slight ear infection, temperature; something that would soon pass.

He took Belenko's temperature, pulse, and blood pressure, then examined his eyes, ears, and throat.

"How do you feel?" he asked.

"Excellent."

"What kind of flight do you have today?"

"Routine exercise."

The physician stopped talking and studied him carefully — skeptically, Belenko thought.

"Tell me, Lieutenant, have you drunk any alcohol in the past twenty-four hours?"

"No, not in the last five days," Belenko answered truthfully.

"Do you think you are ready to fly your mission?"

"I am certain."

"Well, your blood pressure is somewhat high. Nothing to be alarmed about, but for you, rather high. Is something troubling you?"

"Not at all." Anticipating that the body might betray his tensions, Belenko had readied an explanation. "Comrade Doctor, if I don't exercise, I feel like lumpy potatoes, and I've been cooped up for almost a week. This morning, when I saw the sun, I went out and ran like a deer, more than six kilometers. I'm probably still a little winded."

The doctor nodded. "That could account for it. Good luck on your flight, Comrade Lieutenant."

Belenko joined other pilots, who, pending the latest report from the meteorological officer, were standing around the hangar, joking about the forthcoming Communist Weekend. It was preposterous to cover the bunkers with sod. Obviously the Americans long ago had located and targeted the airfield. How could anyone think they would believe it suddenly was not there anymore? Someone said, "Besides, I heard that the cameras in their satellites can photograph a soldier's boots from three hundred kilometers up."

The conversation ceased, and the pilots edged off in different directions at the sight of Vladimir Stepanovich Volodin, the young KGB lieutenant assigned to the regiment. "Good morning, Viktor Ivanovich, how are you?"

"Very well."

"And Ludmilla and Dmitri. How are they?"

"They are well also."

"What's new? What do you hear?"

"Well, the men rebelled again this morning, refused to eat breakfast."

"Yes, I heard. What do you think the problem is?"

Answer him just as you regularly would.

"Vladimir Stepanovich, you know what the problem is as well as I do. Everybody knows."

"I still would like to talk to you. Stop by this afternoon after your flight. Let's talk."

There was nothing at all unusual about this. The KGB officer naturally slinked around, asking, "What's new? What do you hear?" Yet for a moment Belenko worried. *Why did he come to me just now? Why did he ask me that? Well, so what? The bastard won't be seeing me this afternoon, that's for sure.*

The meteorological officers reported that to the east, where Belenko's squadron would fly, the skies were fair and should remain so throughout the afternoon. However, to the southeast, where his actual objective lay, some cloud formations were gathering. A front might be moving in from Japan, but it was nothing to worry about this afternoon.

No! The forecast was clear everywhere. Idiots! How thick is it? Think of a reason to ask him. No, don't. There is no reason. Careful. Show no concern. You'll just have to take the chance.

From the supply room Belenko drew his flight helmet, oxygen mask, and gloves. "Comrade Lieutenant, you forgot your life preserver," a sergeant called. *Don't take it. Fool them.*

"Thanks. I won't be over water today."

Striding from the hangar, he saw the aircraft—twenty MiG-25s—poised wing to wing on the runway some 200 yards away. Weighing twenty-two tons, with twin tail fins, cantilevered tail planes, thick, short, swept-back wings, two enormous engines, and a long rocketlike nose ending with a radar needle, the MiG-25 reminded Belenko of a great steel bird of prey, dark gray and angry. Few weapons in the Soviet arsenal were more closely guarded from foreign observation, and even among themselves the Russians in official terminology simply referred to the MiG-25 as Product No. 84. A stripped-down model in 1967 set a world record by achieving a speed of 1,852 miles an hour, and another in 1973 eclipsed altitude records by soaring to 118,898 feet. Aging American F-4 Phantoms, though equipped with excellent missiles and flown by skilled pilots, had been unable to intercept or shoot down MiG-25s which occasionally streaked over the Mediterranean and the Middle East, taking photographs. No Westerner ever had been close to a MiG-25, and much about it was unknown. Nevertheless, the MiG-25 in the autumn of 1976 was the one plane most feared in the West. In 1973, U.S. Air Force Secretary Robert C. Seamans, a scientist with impressive aeronautical credentials, had characterized it as "probably the best interceptor in production in the world today." While Defense Secretary, James R. Schlesinger had warned that the MiG-25 was so formidable that its widespread development and deployment would force fundamental changes in Western strategy and weaponry. More than 400 of the interceptors had already been deployed. They embodied the most advanced aeronautical technology and, in a sense, the national pride of the Soviet Union. The comparatively few young men chosen, trained, and entrusted to fly them represented an acknowledged and honored elite in the Soviet armed forces.

Swarms of men were making the planes ready. Trucks filled each with fourteen tons of jet fuel and half a ton of coolant alcohol and pumped oxygen into life-support systems. From smaller trucks bearing electronic test equipment, technicians checked the missiles, fire control, and electronic systems. Others stepped under and around the planes, physically inspecting the exterior surfaces and controls.

Belenko climbed a fourteen-foot metal ladder, followed by his flight engineer, who helped him settle into the green cockpit, green because Soviet researchers believed it the most soothing color. The cushioned seat was the most comfortable in which he ever had sat. The various dials, gauges, buttons, and levers were well arranged and easily accessible. Conspicuous among them was a red button labeled "Danger." Pilots were instructed that should they be forced down or have to eject themselves from the aircraft outside the Soviet Union, they must press the button before leaving the cockpit. Supposedly it activated a timing device which a few minutes later would detonate explosives to destroy the most secret components of the plane. Some fliers wondered, however, whether a press of the button might not instantly blow up the entire aircraft, pilot included. He also dared not touch the radar switch because the impulses from the MiG-25 radar were so powerful they could kill a rabbit at a thousand meters. Hence, it was a crime to activate the radar on the ground.

Turning on his radio, Belenko spoke to the control tower. "This is Number Oh-six-eight. Request permission to start engines."

The tower answered quickly. "Number Oh-six-eight, you have permission to start engines."

"Understood. I am executing," Belenko said, waving to his flight engineer, who backed down the ladder, ordered the ground crew to remove the engine covers, and signaled that the hydraulic systems were functioning. As Belenko flicked switches and pushed buttons, the engines produced a soft whine that soon swelled into a roar. "This is Oh-six-eight," Belenko radioed the tower. "I request permission to taxi."

"Oh-six-eight, you have permission."

"Understood. I am executing."

Belenko taxied the MiG-25 to the end of the taxi ramp about half a mile away. Four MiGs were ahead of him, and he had to wait until a green light authorized him to turn onto the runway. "This is Oh-six-eight. Request permission to take off."

"Oh-six-eight, you have permission."

"Understood. I am executing."

He hesitated a few seconds to look once more at the surrounding forests. Above all else in his homeland, he loved the rugged, open expanses and the forests where he had wandered since boyhood. There he could explore and discover and meditate, be alone with a girl or with himself. Only there and in the cockpit had he ever felt free. Under brilliant sunshine, the leaves were turning copper, gold, and ruby, and he thought that the forest never had appeared more majestic, never more impervious and antithetical to human squalor.

With ignition of the afterburner, the aircraft vibrated, bucked, and strained forward. "Oh-six-eight, you have afterburn," the tower confirmed. "We wish you all good." Belenko released the brakes at exactly 12:50 P.M., and the MiG surged down the runway and within fifteen seconds into the air. While still perilously low, he shut off the afterburner prematurely to conserve fuel, which was precious, so precious that he gladly would have exchanged some of his own blood for extra fuel. Also to conserve, he ascended more slowly than usual to 24,000 feet and took five minutes instead of the normal four to enter Training Zone No. 2 on a course of 090 degrees. Beginning the wide 360-degree turn which ground controllers were expecting of him, he saw numerous other MiG-25s in the area, fully armed and fueled. The needle, rotating swiftly around the compass dial with his continuous change in heading, showed that he rapidly was approaching the point of no return. For upon completion of the circle, he would have to proceed either with the programmed flight or with his own.

You can still go back, and nobody will know. If you go, it's forever. I'm going.

Now he began his own secret flight plan.

Back on a course of 090, he let the plane glide downward, hoping the descent would be so gradual the radar controllers would not at once notice. At 19,000 feet, Belenko suddenly jammed the stick forward and to the left and plunged the MiG into a power dive toward the floor of a valley ahead, shrieking and hurtling straight down so that the whole earth seemed to be jumping right into his face until he managed to level off at 100 feet. Never had he attempted such a dive, nor had he ever tried to fly a MiG-25 so low, for below even 1,000 feet it was clumsy and difficult to control. Yet from study of American tactics in Vietnam, he knew that at 100 feet he would be safe

Into the Unknown

from the thickets of SAMs (surface-to-air missiles) and anti-aircraft batteries emplaced on the peaks of the valley and that these bristling peaks would hide him from radar.

Applying power, he thundered through the valley and in two minutes shot out over the Sea of Japan. He pushed an emergency button which started broadcasting a continuous signal indicating his plane was on the verge of crashing. After about forty seconds he turned off the signal to persuade all listening on the distress frequency that it had crashed. Simultaneously he shut down his radar and all other equipment whose electronic emissions might be tracked. Lastly, he switched off his radio, even though it gave off no emissions. He did not want to be affected or distracted by what they might be saying, what they might be doing, how they might be pursuing. He needed now to concentrate purely and intently on the equations of fuel, speed, altitude, time, and distance, which he calculated mainly in his head, aided by only a pencil and tablet. Perhaps use of the cockpit computer would have been more practical and efficient. But he was resolved, as he had done in all crises of his life, to rely on, to trust only himself.

To evade detection by the long-range radars back on land and the missile-carrying Soviet ships patrolling offshore, Belenko flew so low that twice he had to swerve to avoid hitting fishing vessels. Only when he perceived that the waves were rising so high that he might smash into one did he go to a slightly safer altitude of 150 feet.

Along with mounting waves, he encountered darkening skies and rainsqualls which buffeted the plane and portended worsening weather ahead. His mental computations portended much worse. At sea level the MiG was devouring fuel at a fatally gluttonous rate, far exceeding preflight estimates. Rapid recalculations yielded the same grim results. Unless he drastically reduced fuel consumption at once by assuming an altitude of at least 20,000 feet, he never would make landfall. Yet he had not flown far enough to go up safely to that height. He still would be within reach of Soviet radars and SAMs. He also might be picked up on the radars of other Soviet aircraft hunting to rescue him, had he survived a crash at sea, or to kill him, were he still aloft.

Better possible death than certain death, Belenko reasoned, pulling up into the clouds, which quickly encased him in darkness. He had flown on a southeasterly course, dead reckoning his way toward Hokkaido, the northernmost of the Japanese islands and the one closest to his base. At approximately 1:20 P.M.—just thirty minutes after takeoff—he figured he was nearing Japanese airspace and interception by Phantom fighters of the Japanese Air Self-Defense Force. To signify lack of hostile intent and facilitate interception, he throttled back the engines and glided down toward Japan, scarcely sustaining airspeed. Each moment he hoped to break free of the clouds and into the clear, where the Phantoms could see him.

For years he had been taught to fear and fight these planes created by the Americans. Now he awaited them as saving angels. His whole flight plan was predicated upon confidence that the Japanese would scramble fighters to force him down as soon as he intruded over their territory. He knew that the Russians were under orders to fire SAMs at any foreign aircraft violating Soviet territory, and he feared the Japanese would do the same unless he were met and escorted by their own interceptors. More important, he counted on the Japanese interceptors to lead him to a safe landing field. On an old map of Hokkaido he had discerned only one field, the military base at Chitose, which seemed large enough to accommodate a MiG-25. Perhaps the Japanese would lead him to a closer field unknown to him. Regardless, he probably had enough fuel to reach Chitose if they escorted him there promptly and directly. But they would have to find him on their own because his radio frequency band was so narrow he could communicate only with other MiGs.

Thrice during the descent the MiG sliced through thin layers of blue only to be engulfed anew in swirling dirty gray clouds, and not until it had dropped to 1,800 feet did Belenko find himself in clear sky. He circled, attempting to take visual bearings and locate Japanese interceptors. Nowhere could he see an aircraft of any type. *Where are the Phantoms? Where are the damned Phantoms?*

Both Phantoms and MiGs at that moment were all around, desperately searching for him. His plane first appeared on Japanese radar screens as an unidentified blip at 1:11 P.M. when he rose from the sea to 20,000 feet. Nine minutes later, with the blip moving toward the center of the screens, the commander of the Chitose base ordered Phantoms to take off for interception. Simultaneously the Japanese vainly tried to warn him away through broadcasts in both Russian and English. At 1:22, about the time he himself figured, Belenko breached Japanese airspace, and the Phantoms, vectored from the ground, closed upon him. However, at 1:26, as Belenko started to drift down in quest of clear sky, his MiG disappeared from the radarscopes, which, because of worsening atmospheric conditions, were already cluttered with confusing reflections from land and sea surfaces. Without any more guidance from the ground, the Phantoms flew about futilely in the overcast. Almost certainly, Soviet monitors heard the Japanese broadcasts and concluded that the plane being warned was Belenko's, for unidentified aircraft, presumably Russian, streaked toward Japan.

Ignorant of both the Japanese and the Soviet actions, Belenko had no time to conjecture about what might be happening. Neither did he have time for fear.

The Japanese aren't going to find you. At least, you can't count on them anymore. You'll have to take a chance. You have to decide, right now.

From the configuration of the coastline, initially visible to him about 1:30, he deduced that he was approaching Hokkaido's southwestern peninsula. Chitose lay to the northeast, roughly toward the middle of the island, behind a range of mountains still shrouded in clouds. The gauge indicated he had sufficient fuel for another sixteen to eighteen minutes of flight, maybe enough to carry him to Chitose if he immediately headed there. If he went back up into the clouds and over the unfamiliar mountains, however, he would forfeit all control of his fate. Only by sheer luck might he discover a hole in the clouds that would enable him both to descend safely and to sight the military field before exhausting his fuel. Without such good luck, the probabilities were that he would crash into some invisible peak or have to attempt a forced landing on impossible terrain. Had his purposes been different, he might have considered probing for a safe passage downward until his fuel was gone, then bailing out. But to Belenko, preservation of the MiG-25 was more important than preservation of his own life, and he was determined to land the plane intact if there was any chance, even one in a thousand.

Hence, he decided to stay beneath the clouds, fly eastward past the southern end of the mountain range, then turn north toward Chitose. He appreciated that he did not have enough fuel to follow this circuitous course all the way to the air base. But so long as he could see, there was a possibility of finding some place, a stretch of flat land, a highway perhaps, to try to land.

A red warning light flashed in the cockpit at 1:42, and an instant afterward a panel lit up, illuminating the words "You Have Six Minutes of Fuel Left." Belenko reached out and turned off the warning lights. Why be bothered? He was over water again, having crossed the peninsula above Volcano Bay, so he banked into a ninety-degree turn northward toward land, still flying at 1,800 feet. Straight ahead he saw another mass of clouds, but he elected to maintain altitude and plunge into them. They might form just an isolated patch, and the lower he went, the more rapidly the MiG would consume fuel, and the less his glide range would be.

Suddenly a dulcet female voice startled him. Emanating from a recording he did not know existed, the voice was as calm as it was sweet: "Caution, Oh-six-eight! Your fuel supply has dropped to an emergency level. You are in an emergency situation."

Belenko replied aloud, "Woman, wherever you are, tell me something I don't know. Tell me where is that aerodrome."

The fuel gauge stood at empty, and Belenko guessed he had, at most, two minutes left. The clouds had not dissipated, and there was nothing else to do. So he pointed the MiG-25 down toward land and the unknown.

Viktor's Quest

Why? Of all officers, why Belenko? Nowhere in the recorded history of his life and career was an answer discernible. None of the conventional causes that might motivate a man to abandon homeland, family, comrades, and privilege could be found. Belenko was not in trouble of any kind. He never had associated with dissidents or manifested the least ideological disaffection. Like all Soviet pilots, he underwent weekly medical examinations, and physicians repeatedly judged him exceptionally fit, mentally and physically. He drank moderately, lived within his means, was involved with no woman except his wife, and had the reputation of being honest to the point of fault.

In their initial consternation, the Russians did not believe, indeed, could not bring themselves to believe, that Belenko had vanished voluntarily. They preferred to think that he had been lured by invisible forces beyond his control. In a way they were correct, for Belenko was a driven man. And in his flight from the Soviet Union, he was continuing a quest that had motivated and dominated most of his life, a quest that caused him also to ask why.

Belenko grew up as a child alone, left to chart his own course according to destinations and bearings fixed by himself. He was born on February 15, 1947, in a mountain village between the Black and Caspian seas, about a year after his father's release from the Soviet Army. His father had been conscripted in December 1941 at age seventeen, eventually promoted to sergeant, trained as a saboteur and assassin, then assigned to help lead partisan forces. Thereafter he fought with partisans behind German lines, swimming for his life across icy rivers, hiding in frozen forests, and witnessing the slaughter of numberless comrades by enemy patrols, which in combat with irregulars neither gave nor received any quarter. Combat hardened him into a physically powerful, blunt, strong-willed man concerned with little other than survival and the pursuit of women.

When Viktor was two, his father divorced his mother, took him away to the Donbas, the great mining region of southwestern Russia, and subsequently prohibited her from seeing him. They shared a hut with another woman until his father quit her, consigned him to the care of his own mother and sister, and departed for a job 5,000 miles away in a Siberian factory managed by a wartime friend.

The grandmother and aunt lived in one of some forty mud and straw huts that constituted a village near Mine No. 24. Coal dust darkened every structure of the village and so permeated the atmosphere that after a storm temporarily purified the air, food tasted strange. The women occupied one room of the hut and built a bed for Viktor in the other, where they cooked and ate. His aunt rose daily at 5:00 A.M. to draw water from the communal well, stoke the fire, and prepare soup and bread for breakfast before she walked to the mine. There she worked from 7:30 A.M. to 6:00 P.M., sorting debris and alien particles from coal passing on a conveyer belt. She had no gloves, and often her hands were bruised or bleeding. His grandmother, in her seventies, hobbled about with a stick during the day, acting as a good Samaritan, visiting the sick and elderly and attending to an invalid widow who received no pension. Each evening she chanted long litanies before an icon in the corner.

Winter confined Viktor to the hut because, until he was

six, he had no shoes. From the sleeves of an old jacket his aunt sewed slippers useful for dashes to the outhouse but unsuitable for prolonged wear in snow. Incarcerated alone, he could amuse himself only by the exercise of his own imagination and curiosity.

A few days after his fourth birthday Viktor sat close by the stove, a source of both warmth and mystery. What made it yield such good warmth? To find out, he slid open one of the portals, and a burning coal tumbled out onto the straw covering the clay floor. As the hut filled with smoke, he sought escape by crawling into his grandmother's bed and burying himself under blankets. Smoke still bellowed from the hut when he regained consciousness outside, lying in the snow and coughing under the watch of the neighbors who had rescued him. That evening, after they had scrubbed and straightened the hut, his grandmother said, "Viktor, God is watching over you."

During warm weather Viktor wandered and explored, unrestrained, with older boys. A favorite playground was a forbidden area in the woods off the main road between the village and the mines. Here retreating German troops had made a determined stand, and although some nine years had passed, the battlefield had not been entirely cleared. Among trenches and revetments there could still be found live rifle and machine-gun bullets, which the boys used to make firecrackers to scare "witches"—that is, women who scolded them—and small "bombs" for killing and surfacing fish in the river.

Digging for bullets, they unearthed a large, flat, cylindrical object that seemed to them an authentic treasure—one that could be smelted down for thousands of slingshot pellets. Building a bonfire, they gathered around to begin the smelting. The fire waned, and Viktor, being the youngest, was ordered to gather more wood. As he returned, the land mine exploded, hurling him against a tree and causing a severe concussion. Hours later he awakened in the arms of his grandmother, who said with conviction, "You see, Viktor, it is as I said. God is watching over you." The blast had killed two of his friends and badly crippled a third.

That same spring Viktor heard commotion and what sounded like wailing outside the hut. People were gathering in the street, mostly women but some older men also, commiserating with one another, weeping and sobbing, a few hysterically. "Our savior and protector is gone!" a woman moaned. "Who will provide for us now?" The news of the death of Joseph Stalin had just reached the village. Always portrayed by every Soviet medium as a kind of deity, Stalin was so perceived in the village—the military genius who had won the war, the economic genius who had industrialized a feudal society, the political genius who had liberated the Soviet people from capitalist slavery, the just and benign patriarch who had secured the welfare of all.

Accidents frequently took lives in the mines, so Viktor was familiar with mourning and funerals. He had always seen the villagers confront death with stoic restraint, and their bravery added to his regard of the miners as heroic men who risked their lives for the Mother Country. But never had he experienced such unrestrained outpouring of grief and despair as now. It alarmed him and made him wonder, too, how life would proceed without the noble Stalin.

A letter in the autumn saddened both his aunt and his grandmother. His father was coming to take him to Siberia. The grandmother sewed a kind of knapsack for him, and they packed it with food, including some smoked meat, to which they never treated themselves. Through a thick December snowfall the women walked with him and his father to the rail station and held each other, then waved as the train pulled away. He never saw either again.

Authorities in the Siberian city of Rubtsovsk had assured his father that the room in the communal apartment for which he had waited forty-two months would be available by December. It was not, and Viktor was sent to stay on a collective farm, or *kolkhoz*, to the south with relatives of his father's friend, the factory manager. The family—father, mother, and four children—was crowded into one room, and his first evening Viktor stared in wide-eyed wonderment as a cow was led into the hut for the night so she would not freeze to death.

Despite the scarcity of space, the family welcomed him as one of their own and, as had his aunt and grandmother, shared with him unstintingly. He soon recognized, however, that the *kolkhozniks* were far poorer than the miners of the Donbas. The collective allocated each family grain for bread on the basis of the number of workdays credited to the household, rather than according to the number of members. The ration for families with very young children or elderly relatives unable to work was thus short. The small salary paid the *kolkhozniks* barely enabled them to buy essential salt, soap, and kerosene. For purchase of shoes, clothing, and other necessities, they depended on proceeds from the sale of milk and produce grown on their tiny private plots, which they tended fervently and carefully. Throughout the winter their diet consisted of bread and milk for breakfast, boiled potatoes, sauerkraut, and bread for dinner and bread and milk for supper. After the cow stopped giving milk, they drank water.

The winter of 1954 was especially severe in Siberia, so cold that frozen birds littered the ground, and in February the cow could not be allowed outside very long even in daytime. The children amused themselves around the wood-burning stove with games of their own design, and Viktor devised the most popular. The hut was inhabited by big reddish-brown cockroaches, which were accepted as legal residents of all peasant homes and hence not necessarily considered repellent. The intricacy of their bodily composition and functioning fascinated Viktor, and he studied them long and curiously. *How did such complicated creatures come to be? Why are they here? What gives them life?* Watching how quickly they skittered about, he conceived the idea of harnessing the cockroaches by attaching threads between them and toy carts carved from wood. After many failed attempts and mangled insects, he succeeded and began to stage races. The competition became such a source of mirth for all that sometimes after supper the father would say, "Well, Viktor, let us have a race."

The spring thaws awakened and changed the *kolkhoz*. The pure air turned pungent with the omnipresent stench of ordure, but radishes, cucumbers, and tomatoes appeared in the garden, and they tasted delicious. Viktor worked in the fields eleven to twelve hours a day alongside other children, women, and older men, in their fifties or sixties, who constituted most of the labor force. The few teenagers among them malingered and caviled, cursing their barren life in general and the paucity of meat in particular. Once Viktor heard an old woman snap at them: "During the war, we were glad to eat grass and acorns and mice and grasshoppers. You should be grateful that things are much better now." It never occurred to him that the toil was onerous. He liked the outdoors, the physical exertion, and the discoveries of how soil, moisture, sun, and time transform seed into wheat. For a boy of seven it was a pleasant summer.

His father retrieved him in September and in effect appointed him housekeeper of their room on the second floor of a frame apartment building housing employees of the Altai truck factory in Rubtsovsk. His duties included some shopping, preparing a cold supper, cleaning the room, keeping the coke fire burning, and hauling water twice daily from a well about 150 yards down the street. Straining with the pails of water, he remembered the *kolkhoz* and in a few days built a yoke that enabled him to carry two buckets simultaneously. After slipping on winter ice, he constructed a crude, yet serviceable sled to transport water and other cargo. He did not object to the chores any more than he had minded the work on the farm. Rather, from them he gained a sense of partnership and worth, and he prided himself in their accomplishment.

His father went out often in the evening and on Sundays to visit women, and they talked mostly during supper or while playing chess (which, by unspoken agreement, they quit after

Viktor started winning easily). Only once did his father ever discuss his future with him. "You will find your own way in life. I have no friends or relatives in the Party who can help you. I cannot give you money to buy your way out of Rubtsovsk. If you wish a life different from mine, you can find the way only through education. The war took away my opportunity for an education. You still have a chance."

Viktor needed no encouragement. Schooling excited him from the outset and offered, so he thought, the opportunity to learn the answers to all questions about life. And it was through school that he sought an answer to the first question about Soviet life that ever seriously troubled him.

In wartime desperation, the Russians had quickly transfigured Rubtsovsk from a placid market town into a raw, roaring industrial city by transferring factories threatened by the Germans in the west. The forced industrialization was effected mainly by prison labor, and a web of concentration camps developed around the city. Although many camps were closed after Stalin died, those around Rubtsovsk remained, and their inmates were utilized in industrial construction with something akin to wartime urgency. Barbed-wire fences, watchtowers, and lights were erected around construction sites, and shifts of prisoners, or *zeks*, as the Russians called them, were trucked in to keep the work going twenty-four hours a day.

Viktor first sighted some *zeks* while leaning into a stinging wind on the way to school. They were shivering and huddled against one another for warmth inside wire cages on the back of trucks, guarded by Central Asians clad in heavy sheepskin coats and armed with submachine guns. The thin cloth coats, painted with white numerals; the canvas boots; the cloth caps partially covering their shaved heads—all were ragged.

He had seen people in dirty, tattered clothes before. Never had he seen eyes so vacant. There was no expression; it was as if he were looking at men whose minds and souls had died while their bodies continued to breathe. The concept of political prisoners was unknown to him. Criminals were criminals, and he was sure that each of the gaunt, trembling, hollow figures he saw must have done something terrible. Yet he cried out to himself, *Kill them! Kill them or set them free! I would not treat a rat like that. I would rather die than be in a cage.*

His recurrent vision of the *zeks* subsequently caused him to wonder: *Why are they so rejected? What made them that way?* In time, as schools taught him the verities of Marxism-Leninism, he felt he understood. Man, political instructors emphasized, is but the product of his social and economic environment. Capitalism, although a necessary stage in human evolution, created an inherently defective socioeconomic environment based on selfishness, greed, and exploitation of the many by the few. Given such a defective environment, defective human behavior was inevitable. The criminality, alcoholism, acquisitiveness, indolence, careerism, and other aberrant behavior that admittedly persisted in the Soviet Union to some limited extent were merely the malignant remnants of capitalism.

Viktor still pitied the *zeks* but now understood them for what they were—unfortunate victims of the lingering influences of decaying capitalism. Although the past could not be altered, nor their plight remedied, the misery they personified eventually would end with the advent of True Communism.

Shortly before Viktor's tenth birthday his father married a co-worker, the widow of a friend killed in an assembly-line accident. They moved in with her, her mother, sixty-eight, son, six, and daughter, three. She owned a house, a real stucco house consisting of three rooms and a kitchen, well built by her late husband and his relatives on a small parcel of land her parents had been permitted to keep. The outhouse was only a few paces away in the backyard, and the well less than a minute's walk down the block.

The stepmother was a plump, shapeless woman of thirty-five, slightly cross-eyed, and she wore her lusterless hair swept straight back into a tight little bun, a style that emphasized the plainness of her face. Formerly a teacher, she managed both her accounting job at the factory and the household well, for she was by nature efficient, industrious, and, Viktor thought, conniving. He disliked her instantly and, while treating her civilly, gave her no cause to be fond of him.

Despite his father's admonitions, he addressed her formally as Serafima Ivanovna, refusing ever to call her Mother or even Serafima. One Sunday their soup contained meat, which he perpetually craved, but he said nothing when his eye caught her deftly ladling out larger portions of meat into the bowls of her own children. Always he had asked his father for spending money to buy a hockey stick, soccer ball, books, or whatever. Now his father required that he ask Serafima Ivanovna, and usually she declined, politely explaining that the family budget at the moment could not accommodate any frivolities.

Looking for a pencil after school, he found some of her papers and records, studied them, and made a discovery. She was maintaining two bank accounts. Into one she put all of his father's salary and part of her own for general family use; into the other she sequestered some of her salary for the separate benefit of her children. That evening Viktor confronted her with his findings, and during the shouting, abusive argument that ensued, their mutual animosities spilled out. In front of the family Viktor's father took off his belt and flogged him furiously for three or four minutes until his own exasperations were spent. Maybe Viktor could have stopped it sooner, had he cried, but he did not.

The next day he enlisted a schoolmate into a compact to run away, south to the sunshine and orchards of Tashkent. Eluding railway police, then an aged conductor, they slipped aboard a train just as it started to roll out of the Rubtsovsk station. The train, however, was headed north, and they got off at a station some fifty miles away. As they attempted to sneak onto a southbound train, police grabbed them by their collars, dragged them into the station, interrogated and beat them. Unable to verify their false identities, authorities interned them in a detention center for orphans and delinquents pending investigation. The second night they escaped into the countryside by scaling a barbed-wire fence and hid on a *kolkhoz* for a few days before venturing back to the railroad station. There the police again caught them, beat them, and dragged them back to the center. Some three weeks later Viktor's father arrived to bring him home. He was calm. "I cannot stop you from running away. But if you do it again, they will put you in reform school. That is like a prison, and once you have been there, you will never be the same. Think about it; you must decide."

Father is happy with Serafima Ivanovna, and they are good for each other. I am a problem for them both. I do not belong with them. Yet I am forbidden to leave. I cannot change what is. So until I am older, I will stay away as much as I can. Then, on the first day I can, I will leave.

The school maintained a superb library with a large collection of politically approved classics. The room was warm and quiet, and it became a sanctuary into which Viktor retreated in his withdrawal from home. Pupils were not permitted to choose specific books; instead, the librarian selected for them after assessing their individual interests and capacities.

Viktor wondered about the librarian because she was so different from others. Although elderly, she walked erectly and held her head high, as if looking for something in the distance, and her bearing made him think of royalty. He often saw her walking to or from school alone; he never saw her fraternizing with the other teachers or, for that matter, in the company of another adult. There were stories about her. It was said that her husband had been a *zek* and that many years ago she had come from Moscow, hoping to find him in the camps. Some even said that she herself had been a *zek*. Viktor never knew what the truth was. But whatever her past or motives, the librarian elected to invest heavily of herself in him.

Having questioned him for a while, she said, "Well, tell

me, young man, what interests you? History, geography, science, adventure. . . ?"

"Adventure!" Viktor exclaimed.

She handed him a copy of *The Call of the Wild*, which he brought back in the morning. "You disappoint me," she said. "Why do you not want to read the book?"

"But I have read it."

"Really? Please, then, recite to me that which you read."

His accurate and detailed account of the novel by Jack London evoked from her the slightest of smiles and a nod. "Let us see if you can do as well with these," she said, handing him copies of *Tom Sawyer, Huckleberry Finn,* and *Twenty Thousand Leagues Under the Sea.* "However, do not neglect your studies. You have time for many adventures."

Guided and stimulated by the librarian, Viktor became an omnivorous reader, each book she fed him intensifying his hunger for another. He developed the capability of reading any time, any place light allowed, his concentration unimpaired by conversation, noise, or disturbance around him. And he fell into what was to be a lifelong habit of almost reflexively starting to read whenever he found himself with idle time, whether a few minutes or a few hours.

The authors he read became his true parents, their characters his real teachers and, in some cases, his models. He saw in Spartacus, who had led Roman slaves in revolt, the strengths and virtues he desired in himself. To him, Spartacus was even more admirable than the forthcoming New Communist Man because his worth originated from within himself rather than from his external environment. Then the works of the pioneering French aviator and author Antoine de Saint-Exupéry unveiled to him the brilliant vistas of flight, and the pilots who braved the storms and unknowns of the sky to discover and explore its beauties were his heroes.

Discussing Saint-Exupéry with the librarian, he said he longed to fly.

"Why?"

"I think to fly would be the greatest of adventures. The

sky has no boundaries, no restrictions. There nothing is forbidden."

"You know, Viktor Ivanovich, great adventure can be
found in poetry. Tell me, who is your favorite poet?"

"Lermontov. Absolutely. Lermontov." The great nine-
teenth-century Russian poet was a dashing officer frequently
in official disfavor and sometimes in exile. Viktor admired
him both for his adventurous personal life, which ended in a
duel at age twenty-six, and for his art.

"Here is a collection of his works you might enjoy."

Leafing through it, Viktor noted the lightest of little
checkmarks penciled by a poem that began "An eagle cannot
be caged. . . ."

Subconsciously or otherwise, Viktor tried to emulate the
exploits of fictional characters, and in school he behaved like
a Russian reincarnation of Tom Sawyer and Huckleberry
Finn. Learning in physics class how to create short circuits, he
put out the lights in the entire school on a dark winter afternoon and forced dismissal of class for the rest of the day. In
chemistry class he taught himself to make firecrackers with
timing devices. He thus was able to keep a class popping with
a succession of little surprise explosions while he was inno-
cently far away. Once he stole a key, locked the social philosophy classroom from the inside, and jumped out a second-
floor window, preventing the class from convening for three
hours. He achieved perhaps his best coup by letting loose
fifteen lizards in the Russian literature class. Girls shrieked
and ran, and the equally hysterical female teacher took refuge
from the beasts by jumping atop her desk. Manfully Viktor
volunteered to save them all by rounding up the lizards, and
the grateful teacher reported his gallantry and good citizen-
ship to the school director.

After a hockey game in a park in February 1958, four
boys, considerably larger and three to four years older than
Viktor, now eleven, surrounded him and demanded his
money. Instinctively and irrationally he refused. Before taking his few kopecks, they beat him about the face, ribs, and

kidneys with a brutality unnecessary to their purposes. He lay on the frozen snow for five or ten minutes before gathering strength to make his way home slowly to the censure of Serafima Ivanovna, who remarked about the disgrace of hooliganism.

He tended to his wounds as best he knew how and stayed to himself for several days. He could conceal the pain in his sides but not the bloated discoloration of his face, and besides, he wanted to think. *What would Spartacus do?*

The librarian evinced neither curiosity nor surprise when he asked if there were any books about boxing and physical culture. She came back with a book about each and a third book—about nutrition. Viktor filled a burlap bag with sawdust, hung it from the tree in the backyard, and began methodically, obsessively, to punch the bag according to the books. He ran through the streets, chinned himself on the tree, and, with loud grunts, did push-ups and pull-ups until Serafima Ivanovna admonished him to cease the racket. For once his father interceded in his behalf. "What he is doing is not so bad. Let him go his way."

Emboldened by the unexpected endorsement, Viktor asked Serafima Ivanovna if they could add more protein— meat, fish, eggs, cheese (he had never tasted cheese)—to their daily fare of bread, potatoes, and cabbage. According to the nutrition book, protein was essential to the strength and health of the body, especially growing bodies. "All you ask is expensive and hard to buy," she replied. "We do the best we can; I cannot promise more."

The witch is telling the truth. There is nothing she can do. All right, I will find protein for myself.

The hunt for protein led Belenko into the forest beyond the river that curved along the eastern edge of Rubtsovsk. They may have exaggerated, but old men claimed that the Aley River before the war was so clean you could see plentiful schools of big fish swimming five or six feet below the surface and catch them almost effortlessly. But around the city, continuous pollution from chemicals and factory wastes had turned the river into an open sewer, and the despoilment had eaten into the forest, shriveling flora and leaving a belt of scrubland.

About a thousand yards past the scrubland, Viktor entered heavy underbrush and, after pushing on for another half mile or so, came into a dense primeval forest colored and perfumed by wild flowers. He felt like Fabien, the doomed pilot in Saint-Exupéry's *Night Flight*, who, lost and buffeted in a South American storm, suddenly was lifted out of the blackness of the clouds into tranquil heavens lit by stars. Uncontaminated, uninhabited, silent, and serene, the endless forest imbued Viktor with the same sense of space and freedom he was sure awaited him in the sky. And after school recessed for the summer, he virtually lived in the forest.

With a slingshot he killed birds—mostly sparrows, crows, and quail—that abounded in the forest and roasted them on a spit. He learned to detect birds' nests which often yielded eggs. And he gathered wild blackberries, strawberries, cranberries, and tart little green apples. Some days he came alone and, after gorging himself until he could eat no more, settled in a patch of light and read until darkness. More often he invited friends, most of whom were veritable waifs like him, and just as hungry. They constructed a log lean-to, and from this base ranged out in all directions to hunt and explore; their explorations were rewarded by discovery of a clear stream populated by plump trout.

Between May and September Viktor gained thirteen pounds, and with the resumption of school, he looked forward to presenting himself to the librarian. He expected that she would acclaim him for his growth just as she did for his reading. But she was not there. The new librarian would say only that she had retired and "moved away." To where? None of the other teachers knew, or if they did, they would not say. *Why would she go away without saying good-bye to me? What happened to her?* He never did find out.

Viktor continued to pound the punching bag, to exercise and run, and by December he felt ready to stalk the four assailants who had jumped him the preceding February. He encountered one in the same park where they had beaten him. "I have come to pay you back," he announced. "I am going to fight you. Are you ready?"

The boy tried to shove him away, as if not deigning to take him seriously. With a short, quick left jab, Viktor hit him squarely in the face, and he himself was surprised by the force of the blow. *It is working!* He dazed the boy with a left to the jaw, then a right to the ribs. The teenager tried to fight back, but the blow to the ribs had hurt him. Viktor hit him in the jaw with another left and then, with a right, knocked him down. He got up, and Viktor promptly knocked him down once more, this time with a left hook. "Have you had enough?" Viktor shouted.

"All right, let's stop," said the boy, who was breathing heavily on the ground. He slowly got to his feet, whereupon Viktor, without warning, hit him with all his might in the right eye and felled him a third time.

"I did that so you will understand," Viktor said. "The next time I will kill you."

He caught two of the other three and battered them just as badly. His inability to find the fourth did not matter. He had avenged himself, and the fights, the third of which was witnessed by fifty to sixty students after school, established his reputation as someone who had best be left alone.

It also gained him an invitation to an adolescent party on New Year's Eve, 1958. Everyone was gulping homemade vodka, which smelled like a combination of kerosene and acetone. Although Viktor had never drunk alcohol before, he joined in, partially out of curiosity, partially because he thought drinking was expected of him. After about an hour he staggered outside, unnoticed, and collapsed in the snow. He awakened caked in his own vomit. His head throbbed with both pain and fright born of the realization that, had he lain there another couple of hours, he surely would have frozen to death. In his sickness and disgust he made a vow: *Never will I do this to myself again. Never will alcohol get a hold on me.*

Later he came to enjoy alcohol, particularly wine and beer. But he drank it in circumstances and amounts of his own choosing. The ability to control alcohol, or abstain from it entirely, gave him an advantage over many of his peers at each successive stage in his life, if only by granting him more time and energy than they had for productive pursuits.

On a wintry Sunday afternoon a light aircraft crashed near the truck factory. The wreckage was still smoldering and ambulance attendants were taking away the body of the pilot, wrapped in a sheet, when Viktor arrived. The scene transfixed him, and he stayed long after everyone else had gone. Like a magnet, the wreckage kept drawing him back day after day, and he contemplated it by the hour.

Why did he die? Why did I not die in the fire when the mine exploded? Is there a God who decides who will die and when? They say that God is only the product of superstition and that the whole world happened by chance. Is that so? Do the trees and berries grow, do the cockroaches scoot, does the snow fall, do we breathe and think—all because of chance? If so, what caused chance in the first place?

No, there must be some Being, some purpose in life higher than man. But I do not understand. Maybe that is the purpose in life—to try to understand. The pilot must have tried in the sky. What he must have seen! Someday I will take his place and see for myself. Some way I will give my life meaning. I would rather that my life be like a candle that burns brightly and beautifully, if only briefly, than live a long life without meaning.

This embryonic ethos foreordained Viktor to conflict. He wanted to find meaning, to dedicate himself to some higher purpose, to be all the Party asked. Yet he could no more give himself unquestioningly to the Party on the basis of its pronouncements than he could give himself to his grandmother's God on the basis of her chanted litanies. He had to see and comprehend for himself. As he searched and tried to understand, his reasoning exposed troublesome contradictions between what he saw and what he was told.

His inner conflict probably had begun with the announcement in school that First Party Secretary Nikita Sergeyevich Khrushchev had delivered a momentous and courageous address to the Twentieth Party Congress. The political instructor who gravely reported the essence of the speech suddenly turned Viktor's basic concept of contemporary Soviet history upside down. Stalin, the father of the Soviet people, the modern Lenin, Stalin, whose benign countenance still looked at him from the first page of each of his textbooks, now was revealed to have been a depraved monster. Everything he had heard and read about Stalin throughout his life was a lie. For the leader of the Party himself—and who could know better?—had shown that Stalin had been a tyrant who had imprisoned and inflicted death upon countless innocent people, including loyal Party members and great generals. Far from having won the war, Stalin had been a megalomaniac who had very nearly lost the war.

The revelations so overwhelmed and deadened the mind that for a while he did not think about their implications. But as the teachers elaborated upon the Khrushchev speech and rewrote history, questions arose. *It must be true; else they would not say it. But how could Stalin fool everybody for so long? Khrushchev worked with Stalin for years. Why did it take him so long to find out? Why did he take so long to tell us? If everything the Party said before was untrue, is it possible that what it is saying now is also untrue?*

Khrushchev returned from his 1959 visit to the United States persuaded that corn represented a panacea for Soviet agricultural problems. In Iowa he had stood in seas of green corn rising above his head and seen how the Americans supplied themselves with a superabundance of meat by feeding corn to cattle and pigs. The American practice, he decreed, would be duplicated throughout the Soviet Union, and corn would be grown, as the radio declared, "from ocean to ocean." Accordingly, corn was sown on huge tracts of heretofore-uncultivated land—uncultivated in some areas because soil or climate were such that nothing would grow in it.

But the most stupid kolkhoznik *knows you can't grow corn in Siberia. I have seen it with my own eyes. It is not even a foot high, a joke. How can the Party allow something so ridiculous?*

The effort to amend the laws of nature by decree, combined with adverse weather, resulted not in a plethora of corn but rather in a dearth of all grain, which forced the slaughter of livestock. Serious shortages of meat, milk, butter, and even bread inevitably followed. Nevertheless, the radio continued to blare forth statistics demonstrating how under the visionary leadership of the gifted agronomist Khrushchev, Soviet agriculture was overcoming the errors of Stalin and producing ever-larger quantities of meat, milk, butter, bread, and other foodstuffs.

If we have so much bread, why am I standing in line at four A.M., *hoping I can buy some before it runs out? And milk! There has been no milk in all Rubtsovsk for five days and no meat for two weeks. Well, as they say, if you want milk, just take your pail to the radio. But why does the radio keep announcing something which anybody with eyes knows is not true?*

The population of Rubtsovsk included an abnormally high percentage of former convicts because most inmates of the surrounding concentration camps were confined to the city for life upon completing their sentences. Many were irredeemable criminals habituated to assault, robbery, rape, and murder. Armed with knives or lead taped to the palms of their hands, they killed people for no more than the gold in their teeth and robbed men and women of the clothes off their backs in broad daylight. Innocent citizens lost their lives in theaters or on buses simply because criminals in card games sometimes used as their stakes a pledge to kill somebody, anybody.

One Saturday night Viktor rode homeward from a skating rink on a bus with passengers so jammed together that it was hard to breathe deeply, and he had room to stand on only one foot. At a stop the front and back doors swung open, people poured out as if a dam had burst, and Belenko was swept outside with them. From within the bus he heard a heart-rending scream. "They have cut her up. Police! Ambulance!" Lying lifeless on a seat was a young woman, a large, wet crimson splotch on her thin pink coat. There were no public telephones on the streets, and calls for help had to be relayed by word of mouth or runners. The police arrived about an hour later. They could do nothing except haul away the body.

Viktor examined the newspapers the next day. They did not mention the murder, as he was almost certain they would not, for crimes of violence in Rubtsovsk never were reported. They did report the rising crime rate in Chicago along with the rising production of Soviet industry and agriculture.

Of course, I know there are many criminals in Chicago and everywhere else in capitalist countries. How could it be otherwise? They always are having one crisis on top of another. The people are exploited and poor and hungry and plagued by all the other ulcers of capitalism. We don't need the newspaper to tell us that. We need to know what's going on here.

Why do we have so many criminals, so many people who don't want to live openly and honestly? They say the criminals are the remnants of capitalism. But the Revolution was in 1917. That was nearly half a century ago. All these criminals grew up under communism, not capitalism. Why has our system brought them up so poorly?

Having fractured his wrist in a soccer match, Viktor took a bus to the dispensary for treatment. Although his wrist hurt, he recognized that his condition did not constitute an emergency, and he thought nothing of waiting. Ahead of him in the line, though, was a middle-aged woman crying with pain that periodically became so acute she bent over double and screamed. Her apprehensive husband held her and assured her that a doctor would see her soon. Viktor had been there about an hour when a well-dressed man and a woman appeared. A nurse immediately ushered them past the line and into the doctor's office. The husband of the sick woman shouted, "This is not just! Can't you see? My wife needs help now!"

"Shut up and wait your turn," said the nurse.

If we are all equal, if ours is a classless society, how can this happen? And why do some people get apartments right away, while everybody else waits years? And look at Khokhlov [son of a local Party secretary]. He's a real murderer and robber; everybody knows that, and everybody is afraid of him. But every time he's arrested, they let him go. Why does the Party pretend everybody is equal when everybody knows we are not?

One of Viktor's political instructors, the teacher of social philosophy, genuinely idolized Khrushchev as a visionary statesman whose earthy idiosyncrasies reflected his humanitarian nature and his origins as a man of the people. Khrushchev had freed the people of the benighting inequities bequeathed by the tyrannical Stalin, and by his multifaceted genius was leading the people in all directions toward a halcyon era of plenty. On the occasion of Khrushchev's seventieth birthday the instructor read to the class the paeans published by *Pravda*. Everyone could be sure that despite advancing years, the Party leader retained his extraordinary mental acumen and robust physical vigor. *We are lucky to have such a man as our leader.*

Some months later the same instructor, as if mentioning a minor modification in a Five-Year Plan, casually announced that Khrushchev had requested retirement "due to old age." For a while nothing was said in school about the great Khrushchev or his successors. Then it began. Past appearances had been misleading. Fresh findings resulting from scientific review by the Party disclosed that Khrushchev actually was an ineffectual bumbler who had made a mess of the economy while dangerously relaxing the vigilance of the Motherland against the ubiquitous threats from the "Dark Forces of the West." Under Brezhnev, the nation at last was blessed with wise and strong leadership.

This is incredible! What can you believe? Why do they keep changing the truth? Why is what I see so different from what they say?

Recoiling from the quackery of social studies, Viktor veered toward the sciences—mathematics, chemistry, physics, and especially biology. Here logic, order, and consistency prevailed. The laws of Euclid or Newton were not periodically repealed, and you did not have to take anybody's word for anything. You could test and verify for yourself.

He shifted his reading to popular science magazines and technical journals, to books and articles about biology and medicine, aviation and mechanics. At the time, Soviet students were required to study vocational as well as academic subjects, and those who excelled could participate in an extracurricular club the members of which build equipment and machinery. Viktor designed a radio-controlled tractor which was selected for a Moscow exhibition displaying technical achievements of students throughout the Soviet Union. As a prize, he received a two-week trip to the capital.

The broad boulevards of Moscow, paved and lighted; subway trains speeding through tiled and muraled passages; theaters, restaurants, and museums; ornate old Russian architecture; department stores and markets selling fresh fruits, vegetables, and flowers; traffic and official black limousines—all represented wondrous new sights. Collectively they elated him while they inspired pride in his country and hopeful questions.

Is not the Party right after all? Does not what I have seen prove that we are making progress? Will not all cities someday be like Moscow?

The final morning he joined a long line of men and women waiting four abreast outside the Kremlin to view the perpetually refurbished body of Lenin. The Kremlin, with its thick red walls, stately spires, and turrets, connoted to him majesty and might, and upon finally reaching the bier, he felt himself in the presence of history and greatness. He wanted to linger, but a guard motioned him onward. Leaving reverently, he asked the guard where the tomb of Stalin was. The answer astonished him. They had evicted Stalin from the Lenin mausoleum. *Why, they've thrown him away like a dog!*

While telling his classmates back in Rubtsovsk about Moscow, Viktor heard disturbing news. The KGB had arrested the older brother of a friend for economic crimes. He remembered how admiring all had been the year before when the youth had bribed a Party functionary to secure employment in the meat-packing plant. There, as everybody knew, a clever person could wax rich by stealing meat for sale on the black market, and procurement of the job had seemed like a triumph of entrepreneurship. *He will be imprisoned. He will be one of them in the trucks. He will be a* zek.

The specter shocked Viktor into recognition of a frightening pattern in the behavior of many of his peers. Some had taken to waylaying and robbing drunks outside factories in the evening of paydays. Others had stolen and disassembled cars and machinery, to sell the parts on the black market. A few, sent to reform school for little more than malicious mischief or habitual truancy, had emerged as trained gangsters, who were graduating from petty thievery to burglary and armed robbery.

They are becoming real criminals. They never will be New Communist Men. Nothing is going to fix them. How did our communist society do this to them? I do not understand. But if it can make them that way, it could make me that way. That I will not allow. It is as Father said. I must make my own way. I must start now before it is too late.

Always Viktor had received good marks in school without especially exerting himself. He attended to his homework dutifully but quickly so he could devote himself to his own pursuits. Frequently in class, particularly during political lectures, he read novels concealed behind textbooks. Now he resolved to strive during the remainder of school to earn the highest honors attainable, to obey all rules and laws, to try to mold himself into a New Communist Man. Through distinction, he would find his way out of Rubtsovsk and into the sky.

Faithful to his vows, he disassociated himself from most of his friends, studied hard, and parroted the political polemics, even when he believed them absurd. As part of the final examinations in the spring of 1965, he artfully wrote three papers entitled "Progress of the Soviet System," "Crisis of the Western World," and "Principles of the New Communist Man." They faithfully regurgitated the dogma of the day and were brightened by a few original flourishes of his own. The teacher, who read portions of "Progress of the Soviet System" aloud, commended his selection of the tank as the best exemplification of the supremacy of Soviet technology. Although Viktor achieved his goal in social philosophy, a perfect grade of five, he was not entirely proud because he suspected that not all he wrote was true.

Certainly, his assessment of the crisis of the Western world was valid. The grip of the Dark Forces which controlled governments, policies, events, and the people of Western societies was weakening. The Dark Forces, that shadowy cabal, comprised of the U.S. Central Intelligence Agency, the American military, the Mafia, Wall Street, corporate conglomerates and their foreign lackeys, clearly themselves were in retreat and disarray. Everywhere in the West, signs of decay and impending collapse were apparent.* However, he was not so sure that the progress of Soviet society was as real and fated as his paper asserted. And he personally doubted the perfectibility of the New Communist Man, whose evolution and character he delineated in detail.

Maybe it was guilt that caused him to speak out to his detriment. His Russian literature teacher, in some casual comment, said that light is matter. "Of course it isn't," Viktor interjected. "That's basic physics."

What began as a polite discussion degenerated into an angry argument, and Viktor embarrassed the teacher before her class by opening his physics book to a page that stated light is not matter. She ordered him to report to her at the end of the day.

His excellent work, she noted, ordinarily would entitle him to a grade of five. But literature taught, among other things, proper manners. She could not in good conscience

* Sometimes the Russians also used the term "Dark Forces," which Belenko heard throughout his schooling and military career in the Soviet Union, to denote in a narrower sense only the CIA or American intelligence.

award a perfect mark to a student so unmannerly. The difficulty could be eliminated were he to acknowledge his error, recant before the class, and apologize for his impertinence.

No! Why should I say I am wrong when I am right? In science, at least, you must be honest. I will not be dishonest.

The teacher gave him a grade of four, and as a consequence, he was graduated with a silver medal instead of a gold. Still, he had his academic degree, a diploma certifying him as a Grade 3 Mechanic (Grade 6 being the highest), and a letter from school attesting to his good character and ideological soundness. He also had a plan.

The Soviet Union maintains a military auxiliary, the Voluntary Society for Assistance to the Army, Air Force and Navy, which is known by its Russian acronym DOSAAF. Among other functions, DOSAAF provides young volunteers with technical military instruction preparatory to their entry into the armed services. Viktor learned that the branch in the city of Omsk, 380 miles away, offered flight training. By finding a job in Omsk to support himself, he reasoned, he could learn to fly through DOSAAF.

His farewell to his father and stepmother was awkward, for all pretended to regret that he was leaving home, while each knew that everyone was relieved. His father gave him a note to a cousin living in Omsk and, shaking hands, pressed twenty rubles into his palm. He did not know whether his father wished to conceal the gift from Serafima or whether he simply was too embarrassed to make it openly. He did realize that his father could ill afford the gift, which equaled roughly a sixth of his monthly take-home pay.

Omsk, larger, busier, and colder than Rubtsovsk, was an important center of armament production, a major way-stop on the Trans-Siberian Railway, and a hub of air traffic between Siberia and the rest of the country. When Viktor arrived in June 1965, the factories manufacturing tanks, armored vehicles, artillery, aircraft engines, and other military hardware were running full blast day and night seven days a week, and they continued to operate at the same forced pace as long as he was there. Jobs were plentiful; the problem was finding a place to live. Therefore, his father's cousin steered Viktor to the repair garage of Omsk Airport, which maintained a dormitory and cafeteria for its employees, gave them substantial discounts on airline tickets, and issued them warm work clothing, including heavy jackets and comfortable boots lined with dog fur.

The garage, a cavernous brick hall with an arched tin roof that rattled loudly in the rain, was cold and dark. A dozen mechanics were under the supervision of senior mechanic Igor Andronovich Yakov. He was a big, husky man with thick white hair, a red nose, deep voice, and huge hands calloused by forty years of labor on the roads and in the garages of Siberia. For some three decades he had driven heavy trucks until, after repeated arrests for drunken driving, he finally lost his license. The airport nonetheless was glad to have him as a Grade 6 mechanic because, drunk or sober, he could fix vehicles. He shared his skills with anyone who asked his help, and he could not resist lending money, no matter how many times the borrower had previously defaulted. He was the undisputed and popular boss. And his standing and kindness possibly saved Viktor's life on his first day at work.

About 11:30 A.M. the master welder shoved some money at Viktor and in a patronizing tone said, "Kid, go buy some juice."

"I don't want anything to drink."

"I didn't ask what you want. I told you to go buy vodka."

"No! I won't."

Brandishing a wrench, the welder approached Viktor. By not retreating, he created a confrontation which neither man could back out of except through humiliating surrender.

He will swing from the right. I should duck under to the left. No. If I fail, the wrench will kill me or cripple me.

Viktor jumped at the welder and with a succession of rapid jabs knocked him against the wall and twisted the wrench out of his hand.

He turned and saw three other mechanics coming at him

with wrenches. Stepping left, then right, then backward, he tried to prevent any of them from getting behind him, but they succeeded in maneuvering him toward a corner.

"Enough!" Yakov shouted. "All of you!"

Wielding a wrench of his own, Yakov grabbed Viktor by the arm and, jerking him away, announced, "The young man and I will buy the vodka."

They walked four or five minutes before Yakov spoke. "You realize they would have killed you."

"Maybe I would have killed some of them first."

"And in your grave, would you have been proud? Listen to me, young one; I know. In a socialist society do not be a white crow among black crows; else you will be pecked to death. If you want to be a different kind of bird, never let the others see your true colors."

At Yakov's insistence, Viktor attempted an apology to the welder; it was hard, but he offered his hand, which the welder refused. After they drank awhile, though, he slapped Viktor on the back and shook hands.

Viktor had violated both a daily ritual and a long-standing custom requiring the most junior man to fetch the vodka.

Typically, about 11:30 A.M. Yakov signaled the effective end of the workday. "Well, enough of that business. We can do that anytime. Let's talk real business. I have eighty kopecks. Let's organize something and send the kid. He'll bring us gas."

The ensuing exchanges seldom varied. "I have a ruble."

"I'll support you with seventy kopecks."

"I can't. I have no money today."

"Well, I'll lend you fifty kopecks."

"All right, kid. Take the money, and do your job."

Viktor jogged or ran, which he liked to do anyway, to a store a quarter of a mile away to arrive before the noon crowd formed. His duty was to bring back the maximum amount of alcohol purchasable with the money collected, after he had set aside enough for bread and canned fish. The cheapest vodka cost three rubles sixty-two kopecks a half-liter, and a bottle of Algerian red wine one ruble twenty kopecks; a kilogram of good Russian bread could be bought for sixteen kopecks, and a can of foul-tasting fish for forty kopecks.

Yakov entertained his colleagues by lining up the glasses, shutting his eyes, and, measuring by sound, pouring almost exactly the same amount of vodka or wine into each glass. Glasses filled, the party began and lasted until there was no more to drink. The men then settled by the coal stove to play dominoes, smoke, and tell jokes, allowing only an emergency to intrude on their leisure. The garage manager did not bother them; they accomplished in half a day all that was demanded, his superiors were happy, and by keeping in their graces, he could count on the mechanics if serious need arose.

Viktor in turn empathized with them; he understood that the garage was their prison and that they had given up even dreaming of parole. He realized, too, the meaning of the words that followed Yakov's first swig of vodka. "Ah, this puts a little pink in the day." For him the garage became a comfortable haven from which he could pursue his overriding goal of flight.

Having survived scrutiny of his ideological stability, study of his education, and a rigorous physical examination, Viktor was one of forty young men selected for DOSAAF preflight training. Five nights weekly he hurried from work to the cafeteria, then took a bus across town to DOSAAF offices located in a prerevolutionary bank building. The subjects— aerodynamics, navigation, design and construction of aircraft, radio and electronics, meteorology, and rules of flight—were not inordinately difficult. Many cadets, though, could not manage both the volume of study required and a daily job, and by the end of the first month fully a fourth had dropped out.

Viktor never had been so happy as in DOSAAF classes. They were devoid of cant, pretense, hypocrisy. Defying regulations, the chief instructor omitted the teaching of political theory. Careers and lives might hinge on how much and how well they learned, and there was no time for trivia. The instructors were retired Air Force pilots, and in Viktor's eyes they stood as real men who had braved and survived the skies. They treated the cadets as both subordinates and comrades, as future partners from whom nothing should be hidden. Direct questions to them elicited unequivocal, comprehensible answers, and for any question concerning flight, they had an answer. The closer they led him to flight, the more its challenge engrossed him.

The first parachute jump was scheduled in December, and a parachutist, an Air Force major, readied them for it. He said that although he had jumped more than a thousand times, he still was afraid before jumping. "Do not fear your own fear," he told them. "It is natural." The temperature was forty degrees below zero as Viktor and eight other cadets climbed into the small AN-2 transport at an airfield thirty miles from Omsk. He was not afraid; he was terrified. He felt only like an automaton irreversibly programmed to proceed to its own doom. When the parachutist swung open the door and freezing air rushed and whistled into the cabin, he had to reach into his deepest reserves of strength and will to make himself stand up and take his place, third in line. *Will it open? Will I remember? Am I now to die?*

The parachutist slapped his shoulder, and he plunged headlong into the void. *Remember! Count! Now! Pull!* A tremendous jerk shook his body, and he yelled in exultation. He was suspended, adrift in endless, pure beautiful space; he was free, free from the earth, unfettered to any of its squalor, confusion, pettiness, meanness. He laughed and sang and shouted. *I am being foolish. But what does it matter? No one can hear me. No one can see me. I am free.*

Absorbed in the rhapsodies of the sky, Viktor returned to earth ingloriously, landing squarely on the back of a cow. Under the impact, the startled cow involuntarily relieved herself and bounded away, dumping him in the manure. He only laughed at himself, for nothing could detract from his joy. He wanted to go back up immediately and jump again.

Before, he had longed, hoped, imagined. Now he knew. His future was clear. As long as he lived, he would live to be in the sky.

After written examinations in mid-April, the students met their future flight instructors. Viktor was mortified upon being introduced to his. He had counted on being taught by a real fighter pilot, perhaps one who had flown against the Americans in Korea or Vietnam. Instead, he was assigned to a woman, Nadezhda Alekseyevna, who was about thirty-five. She still had the figure of a gymnast, and despite a rather rough complexion and bobbed hair, she was pretty. It almost would have been better had she been ugly.

The sullenness with which he etched a hollow outline of his background betrayed to her his disappointment. She recognized all the cues of male resentment, for she was one of the few female pilots in DOSAAF, if not the sole one. She had earned her wings and place only through prodigious determination. At age eighteen, she had joined a parachutist club open to women and subsequently finagled her way into a glider club. Through influence in Moscow, she had graduated from gliders to DOSAAF flight training and so excelled that she won grudging acceptance as an instructor. For the past eight years she had taught, always having to be better to be equal, always having to prove herself anew, always having to tolerate the lack of any separate facilities for women at air bases.

"Do you really want to fly?" she asked Viktor.

"Very much."

"All right, we will work on it together. I am proud of many of my students. Some now are fighter pilots. I hope you will make me proud of you."

By law, the garage had to grant Viktor leave of absence with three-fourths pay during his flight training at an airfield north of Omsk. The field had long ago been abandoned by the Air Force to DOSAAF, and it was closed except during late spring and summer. They had to open the mess hall and World War II barracks and keep wood fires burning around the clock because even in early May the temperature was below freezing. Instructors, cadets, Air Force administrators, mechanics, cooks, and guards all joined in clearing the runways of snow and making the base serviceable.

On their first training flight in the YAK-18U, an old, yet excellent trainer easy to handle, Nadezhda Alekseyevna told him, "Place your hand lightly on the stick and throttle and your feet on the rudders. Do not exert any pressure. Just follow my movements." She climbed leisurely to about 5,000 feet. Suddenly she threw the plane into violent maneuvers — dives, an inside loop, an outside loop, barrel rolls, a stall, then a spin. The whole earth was rushing up into Viktor's face to smash him. He did not know what was happening, only that the end was imminent. Persuaded that she had scared him enough, Nadezhda Alekseyevna deftly pulled out, circled, and landed.

Viktor stood uneasily, still adjusting to the ground. "Do you still want to fly?" she asked.

"Yes."

"Do you think I can teach you?"

"I know you can."

"All right, from now on, let's work together like adults."

On their fourth flight, she instructed, "Make a ninety-degree turn to the left." He banked and, pulling out a little late, altered course about 100 degrees but otherwise executed flawlessly. "Okay, ninety degrees to the right." This time he watched the compass carefully and straightened out on a heading exactly ninety degrees from the previous course. "I'm going to put us into a spin and let you try to rescue us." She arched the plane upward and throttled back the power until it stalled, then nosed over into a dizzying spin. "Now it's up to you!"

Easily Viktor pushed the stick forward, stepped on the rudder, halted the spin, and pulled back out of the dive.

"Very good! Try a loop."

Viktor dived, then lifted the plane upward and over and backward into a loop. At the height of the loop, when they were upside down, he snapped the plane into a half roll and righted it, effecting an Immelmann turn, a much more difficult maneuver than could be expected of him.

"Impudent! But good!"

Without instructions, he did a full loop, then a series of quick rolls.

"All right! All right! Let's see if you can land."

Unharnessing their parachutes, Nadezhda, who heretofore had addressed Viktor formally as Viktor Ivanovich, said, "Viktor, you can do it. You have the talent. You can be a great flier."

Everyone else saw it, too. Viktor could fly, as naturally as a fish swims. And to him the sky had become as water is to a fish. Before his first solo flight, he was cocky and, afterward, still cockier. When he landed after his final flight test, the lieutenant colonel who flew in the back seat shook his hand. "Young man, outstanding. I hope we see you in the Air Force."

The instructors and cadets gathered in the mess hall on a Friday night, their last before returning to Omsk, for a great party. Even before vodka began to evaporate inhibitions, Nadezhda abandoned her role as a superior and confided that his performance had won her a commendation. "You have made me proud, Viktor."

In the morning melancholy replaced euphoria as Viktor canvassed his immediate future. It was too late to apply this year for Air Force cadet training. He could continue the nightly DOSAAF classes, but now the theory of flight seemed a pallid substitute for the reality of flight. He would have to subsist during the next months in the dark void of the garage without adventure or meaning. *What a miserable fix. Well, whining won't help you. That is the way it is. Do something about it.*

Returning to Omsk in August, Viktor heard that because the military anticipated need for many more doctors, there would be an unusual number of openings in the fall classes at the local medical school. Out of a whim to test his capacities, he took the entrance examinations. Toward the end of the month the medical school notified him that he ranked near the top of all applicants and advised him to report for enrollment. *Why not? If you could be a doctor as well as a flier, think of all the adventures you could have! One of the cosmonauts is a doctor. If he could do it, why can't you?*

Just three days after medical-school classes convened, they abruptly and unexpectedly were suspended so students could participate in the harvest. Legions of young people from factories, the universities, the Army were being trucked into the countryside. The manufacture of goods, the education of physicians, the training of the nation's guardians must wait. All available manpower had to be mobilized for the frantic, desperate battle of the harvest.

Why are we so unprepared? The harvest is not something that happens only once every twenty or thirty years. It is known that each fall crops must be harvested. Why do we have to tend to the business of the kolkhozniks?

Viktor and some of his classmates were deposited on a *kolkhoz* outside Omsk, hundreds of miles away from the collective where he had stayed as a child in 1954. The years had brought some improvements. The *kolkhoz* manager traveled about in a little car instead of a horse-drawn buggy. Some of the *kolkhozniks* had transistor radios, and once a week they were shown a movie on portable screens. But Viktor could identify no other substantive changes.

The huts, the muddy streets, the stink were the same. The bedraggled work force was composed mainly of the elderly, women, children, half-wits, or men too dull to escape into more prestigious and less onerous jobs at the tractor station or dairy. Abused and neglected, machinery still broke down and rusted. And nobody gave a damn about anything except his small private plot of land that he was allowed to cultivate.

It's all the same. Everything's still messed up. Why, we've made no progress at all. Something is wrong here.

Having been told they would be paid the same wages as the *kolkhozniks*, Viktor expected that since he had spent none of his salary, a nice sum awaited him. However, after deductions for food and lodging in the hut of a widow, his pay for fifty-eight consecutive days of labor, sunup to sundown, totaled thirty-nine rubles forty kopecks. *Exploitation! Why, the* kolkhozniks *are exploited as badly as capitalist workers!*

Relieved as an inmate released from a labor camp, Viktor eagerly immersed himself in his premed courses. All the academic subjects, especially anatomy and biology, fascinated and challenged him. Like teachers everywhere, the professors were stimulated by, and in turn stimulated, the strongest minds, and they favored him with extra attention.

There were problems, however. Political courses of one form or another robbed him of about a third of his academic time. He had heard it all before, ever since the first grade, in fact. *All right! Capitalism is horrible; communism is wonderful. Let us try to make it better by studying. Let us learn how to be doctors. Don't waste our time with all this crap.*

By January 1967 the savings he had accumulated from the unspent salary paid him by the garage during DOSAAF training were nearly depleted, and he obviously could not survive on the monthly stipend of thirty rubles granted medical students. There being no room in the dormitory, his father's cousin generously took him into his small apartment. But his presence added such a conspicuous burden to the overcrowded family that he was ashamed to impose on them much longer.

To afford the family privacy, Viktor usually skated in the park on Sunday afternoons. The pond was crowded, a light snow falling, and he did not recognize the heavily bundled figure waving at him until they were almost upon each other. "Nadezhda!"

"Cadet Belenko! Join me for a cup of tea?"

They went to a state teahouse near the park. Shorn of her wraps, her cheeks pinkened by the cold, Nadezhda looked radiant. She had been in the Caucasus, qualifying herself to fly the Czech L-29 jet trainer. "You haven't flown until you've flown a jet. Everything is different and better: the sound, the feel, what you can do. Why don't you come back to class and learn about jets? If you do, I'll be one of your teachers."

Viktor quit medical school in the morning, registered for DOSAAF classes, and began looking for a job, any job that carried with it a dormitory room. Factory No. 13 had dormitories close by its sprawling facilities, and it was so hungry for people that he was hired on the spot and immediately trundled off, with four other men and two women, for orientation. A young KGB officer solemnly discoursed about the momentous import and honor of the duties they were beginning. Factory 13 was an important defense installation, and all that transpired inside was strictly secret. "If anyone asks what you make, you are to say cookware, toys, and assorted other household hardware."

This is ridiculous. Is every official in the whole Soviet Union not only a liar but a stupid liar?

Everyone in Omsk who cared to know knew what came out of Factory 13, one of the largest plants in the city—tanks and only tanks. How could they not know? More than 30,000 people worked there. When the freight trains failed to come on time and output backed up, you could see the tanks, sleek, low-slung, with thick high-tensile steel armor and a 122-millimeter gun protruding like a lethal snout, parked all over the place. And even after they were loaded on flatcars and covered with canvas, their silhouettes revealed them to be, unmistakably, tanks.

Stepping into the building where wheels and treads were made, Viktor reflexively clamped his hands over his ears. Clanging, banging, strident, jarring noise assailed him from all around, from up and down. It came from the assembly line, from the lathes, and, most of all, from the mighty steam press, forged by Krupp in the 1930s, confiscated from Germany, and transplanted to Siberia. He felt as if he were locked in a huge steel barrel being pounded on the outside with sledgehammers wielded by mad giants. He soon began to perspire because the heat from the machinery, all powered by steam, was almost as overwhelming as the noise.

His section employed approximately 1,000 people in three shifts, and the sheer number of personnel, together with the incessant noise, precluded the kind of easygoing intimacy he had known at the airport garage. There were, however, some distinct similarities.

The dominant subject of conversation among the men was when, where, and how to drink. In the aftermath of accidents and failed quotas, alcohol had been banned from the premises, but workers regularly smuggled in bottles so they could "take the cure" in the morning after a night of heavy imbibing. And with the ban on alcohol, a "factory kitchen" had been opened just outside the plant gate, ostensibly to sell snacks for the convenience of the employees. It actually was a full-fledged, rip-roaring saloon, where, beginning at noon, workers belted down as much vodka as they could afford. If drinking continued inside the plant in the afternoon, custom and prudence necessitated setting aside a hefty portion for the supervisors, who, having become co-felons, retired to their offices for a nap. On payday little work was attempted as excitement at the imminent prospect of limitless drinking mounted, and workers prematurely quit their posts to line up for their money. Quarrels, accompanied by curses, screams, or tears, erupted as wives endeavored to intercept husbands and some money before the drinking began.

His own budget enabled Viktor to appreciate the desperation of the women. Like virtually all other workers at the tank factory, he earned 135 rubles a month, about 15 percent more than the standard industrial wage then prevailing in the Soviet Union.* Some 15 rubles were withheld for taxes, dues,

* The ruble is not traded on international money markets, hence its value does not fluctuate according to supply and demand. The Soviet government fixes the official exchange rate, which in June 1979 was set at $1.50. However, foreign-money brokers reported the same month that they sold the ruble to volume purchasers for as little as 20 cents. An American official who periodically travels to the Soviet Union stated that on the black market in

and room rent; his minimum monthly bus fares amounted to 10 rubles; by eating at the cheapest factory cafeterias and often making sandwiches in his room, he could keep the cost of meals down to 90 rubles. So he had about 20 rubles left for clothing, personal necessities, and recreation. He could manage, but he did not understand how a man with a wife and children managed, especially if he drank vodka every day.

Viktor came to feel that even were the prohibition against alcohol effectively enforced, it would not materially increase production or efficiency. For the attitudes, habits, and work patterns of the men were, as they said, "cast in iron." Most were quite competent at their craft. They worked well and diligently in the morning and, unless machinery broke down, usually fulfilled their quota by noon. But once a quota was met, they ensured it was not exceeded. They would stop the furnace to extract a 200-kilogram mold "which was stuck" or change the stuffing box in the press cylinder because "the steam pressure is too low" or intentionally make something defective so that it would have to be remade.

An ironsmith in Viktor's section was a veritable genius at his work and ordinarily discharged his assigned duties in an hour or so, then loafed the remainder of the day, smoking, strolling about, and chatting with friends. Out of curiosity rather than censure, Viktor frankly asked why he did not make a hero of himself by surpassing his quota, as the Party constantly exhorted everybody to do. "You know nothing of life, young fellow," he replied. "If I chose, I could do ten times as much work. But what would that bring me? Only a quota ten times as high. And I must think of my fellows. If I exceed my quota, they will be expected to exceed theirs."

The Educational Section of the Cultural Division of the tank factory employed ten or eleven artists full time to paint posters intended to correct such attitudes and inspire the

---

Moscow a dollar will buy five or six rubles. Probably the most meaningful way of gauging the worth of the ruble in any other currency is to compute the number of hours a Soviet consumer must work to buy a given item at the prices fixed by the Soviet government.

workers. Some of the posters Viktor saw were labeled "Be a New Communist Man," "Marching Toward True Communism," "Building a New Base for Communism," "I Will Exceed My Quota 100 Percent," "Be a Hero of the Party," "The Party and People Are One." The posters and the weekly political lectures by Party representatives did provide conversation pieces, and a favorite topic they raised was the utopian life True Communism would introduce.

The Twenty-second Party Congress in 1961 had proclaimed that the Soviet Union would largely realize True Communism by 1980. True Communism, by definition, would inundate the land with such a bounty of goods and services, food and housing, transport and medicine, recreational, cultural, and educational opportunities that each citizen could partake of as much of the common wealth as he or she wished. And all would be free! Born of an environment that fully and continuously gratified all material needs, a new breed of man would emerge—the New Communist Man—unselfish, compassionate, enlightened, strong, brave, diligent, brotherly, altruistic. He would be unflawed by any of the imperfections that had afflicted man through ages past. There would be no reason for anybody to be otherwise.

But on the oil-soaked floors of the factory, the assembly-line workers took their indoctrination sessions with more than a great deal of skepticism:

"Since everybody can have as much of everything as he wants and everything will be free, we can stay drunk all the time."

"No, I'm going to stay sober on Mondays because every Monday I will fly to a different resort."

"I will stay sober on Sundays; half sober anyway. On Sundays I will drive my car and my wife will drive her car to the restaurant for free caviar."

"And we won't have to work. The tanks will produce themselves."

"Hey, this New Communist Man, does he ever have to go to the toilet?"

The irreverent mockery of the promised future usually was accompanied by obscene complaints about the real present. Someone's mother still was not being paid the pension to which she indisputably was entitled. The façade of the apartment building had fallen off, and wind was blowing through the exposed cracks. Somebody had been informed he would have to wait another year for the apartment that was supposed to have been his two years ago and for which he already had waited five years. Some son of a bitch had stuffed up the garbage chute again, and the whole building was beginning to stink like a cesspool. Half the meat somebody's wife had stood in line three hours for turned out to be spoiled when unwrapped.

The slogans, exhortations, theories, and promises of the Party were as irrelevant to their lives, to the daily, precarious struggle just to exist, as the baying of some forlorn wolf on the faraway steppes. To the extent they took note, it was to laugh, to jeer at the patent absurdities and hypocrisies. Yet in the tank factory, as on the *kolkhoz* and in the garage, everyone appeared to accept the circumstances against which he inveighed as a chronic and natural condition of life. Never did he hear anyone suggest that the fault might lie within communism itself or insinuate that the system should be changed. And no such thought occurred to Viktor.

At the time, he had never heard of Aleksandr Solzhenitsyn, Andrei Sakharov, or any other dissidents. He had never read a *samizdat* publication or any other illicit writings, nor had he ever heard a foreign radio broadcast. He was unaware that anyone in the entire Soviet Union opposed the system itself, except, of course, the traitors traduced by the Dark Forces.

For all the unconcealable defects, the admitted mistakes of the past, the conspicuous inefficiencies, there was empirical evidence that the system, after a fashion, did work. The harvest, after all, had been gathered. Workers after some years did get apartments. Before holidays, meat and even toilet paper could be bought in the stores. Tanks were manufactured, and as he himself had written, they were the best tanks in the world, and the Soviet Union had thousands of them. Besides, things were worse in the West, where capitalism inexorably was disintegrating in accordance with the laws of history.

There remained in his mind, however, corrosive thoughts that he could not extirpate, contradictions that multiplied doubts while sapping faith. *You can't be sure of anything the Party says. It was wrong about Stalin; it was wrong about Khrushchev. Little that I see is like what it says. We are not equal. Each of us is different, and nothing will ever make everybody the same. There never will be a perfect man. Why, that's ridiculous. The workers know that; everybody knows that. And this new base for True Communism; at the rate we're going, we won't build that for a hundred years, two hundred years. Something's wrong here. I just don't know what.*

Although Viktor did not try to be "a white crow among the black crows" at the factory, he did attract the attention of management. Noticing his mechanical aptitude and how quickly he learned, a supervisor made him a kind of utility man who substituted for absentees, and he became adept at a variety of jobs. Solely because he preferred to do something, anything, rather than lounge about idly, he always was willing to work. Sometimes on Saturday, when there was no DOSAAF class, he did contribute to the purchase of vodka and share a glass or two with his colleagues. Otherwise, he did not drink on the job, and he never showed up incapacitated with a hangover.

One morning in April his supervisor told him to report to the office of the factory manager. Also present were a Party representative, who was part of management, and the deputy personnel director, who probably was a KGB officer. The manager, an earnest man, stated that the factory required engineers combining the talents and personal qualities he exemplified. Therefore, the factory was willing to send him to a university to study industrial engineering for five years. It would pay him three-fourths of his present salary, plus an allowance for food, lodging, and travel. Because the factory was a vital defense installation and in light of his DOSAAF training, he would be exempt from military service. In return, he would have to commit himself to work at the factory for at least two years after his graduation. The manager said he realized that the offer was a surprise and that he wanted him to ponder his answer carefully. He would need an answer by June.

The honor and opportunity were enormous, and to almost any young man of his status, the offer would have been irresistible, as it was intended to be. Out of politeness, Viktor thanked the manager and promised to deliberate in the coming weeks. To himself, he instantly answered no. *This is a swamp, and it will trap you, and you never will escape. I would live a little better than the workers, but for what purpose would I live? Here there is no meaning, no hope, nothing to look forward to.*

Outside the factory Viktor did have something to look forward to—the possibility of entering the Air Force in the fall and, every week or so, a few hours with Nadezhda. From her manner in class no one would have discerned that they knew each other personally. But on Sundays, when they skated, attended a hockey match or the theater, to which she once invited him, or merely walked in the park and drank tea, neither disguised their liking for the other.

Toward the end of the month she called him aside before classes began. "Pay close attention tonight. This may be your chance."

There was a special speaker, a colonel who had come to solicit applications for the Soviet Air Defense Command flight-training program conducted at Armavir in the Caucasus. The colonel was candid and businesslike in his briefing. Khrushchev believed that rockets alone could defend against aircraft, and consequently, he had cashiered thousands of fighter pilots who now were dispersed in civilian life, their skills rusted by disuse. The performance and tactics of American aircraft in Vietnam increasingly proved that Khrushchev was wrong. Valuable as missiles were, aircraft also were essential to combat aircraft. The Mother Country required a new generation of fighter pilots to rebuild its interceptor forces. Only the best would be chosen; their training would be long and arduous. But for those who succeeded, the career opportunities, material rewards, and honor of joining the elite of the Soviet armed forces would be great. Selected applicants would report to Armavir in June for the examinations that would determine whether they were admitted to the program.

The colonel in charge of DOSAAF helped Viktor prepare an application the next evening and forwarded it with an ardent endorsement. Two weeks later the colonel informed him he had been accepted for the examinations.

Viktor took three bottles of vodka with him to say good-bye to the men with whom he had worked at Factory 13. They congratulated and toasted him; sincerely, he was sure. After two bottles were gone, they sent for more vodka, and as he left, the celebration was growing more boisterous.

In a few hours, their happiness will evaporate, and they will be lost again in the swamp. Their lives are over. Something is wrong; I don't know what.

The
First
Escape

An overpowering, unrelenting stench saturated the unventilated coach, emanating from its filthy toilet, from the vomit of drunks, from bodies and clothes too long unwashed. The windows, grimy and flyspecked, could not be opened. And the unupholstered wooden benches of the coach, with their high, straight backs, made any posture miserable. Yet the very squalor of the train sustained him by reminding him that he was journeying away from squalor.

On the fifth morning he awakened from a half sleep and saw that during the night the train had entered the rich plains surrounding Armavir. Under the yellow sunshine they were moving through fields of green wheat, then past blooming orchards and vineyards. Bounding from the train as if springing out of a cage, he delighted in the comparative cleanliness, warmth, and gaiety of Armavir. It was an old city with cobblestoned streets, trees, flowers, and a number of colorful prerevolutionary buildings that had withstood war and social change. Among the 200,000 inhabitants were substantial numbers of indomitable Armenians and Georgians and an abnormal proportion of pretty girls, many of whom attended a nursing school or teachers' college.

The clime was balmy and benign, and wanting to exercise, Belenko jogged to the camp for applicants eight miles outside the city. A spirit of high expectancy and camaraderie pervaded the throngs of young men he joined there. They had traveled from all reaches of the Soviet Union, more than 4,000 of them, lured and united by the hope that they would be chosen to fly. No one told them that the slightest physiological flaw, no matter how irrelevant to health or flying, would disqualify them. No one told them that survivors of the physical scrutiny would have to score almost perfectly on the written tests to have a chance. No one told them that out of the thousands, only 360 would be selected. Consequently, they talked of imminent glories and rewards in the sky, never acknowledging that they might be among the rejected, condemned to two years of harsh servitude as common soldiers. Few complained about the drudging tasks assigned them while they waited their turn to be examined—unloading bricks, digging ditches, laying concrete slabs for runways, weeding fields. This was a small price.

Physicians inspected, probed, pressed, X-rayed, tested, interrogated, and listened to Belenko for five days; then one stamped his medical records "Fit for Flight Training Without Restrictions." For him, the written examinations assessing basic knowledge of the sciences and Party theory were easy, and he did well. When the names of the first 180 successful candidates were posted in alphabetical order the last week of June, his was there.

The morning Belenko was formally sworn into the Soviet armed forces, a squat sergeant, the right side of his face jaggedly scarred almost from ear to chin, lined him and nineteen other cadets into a squad. Pacing the line, he put his face close to that of every second or third cadet, glowered, and sniffed like a dog. Belenko thought he was either slightly daft or trying to be funny. Suddenly the sergeant stepped back and commenced to revile them, obscenely and furiously. "So, you dripping chickens, you're in the Soviet Army, and I'm going to tell you something about our Army. They say that life in the

Soviet Army is like life in a chicken coop. You know you're going to get screwed; you just don't know when, how, and by whom. Well, I'll tell you when—whenever you do anything different from what I say. You obey me absolutely, day and night, or I'll have your head as well as your ass. We have another saying. The chicken began to think and wound up in the soup, shit soup. From now on, I think for you. You will think, you will behave, you will look just as I say. Look at your miserable selves; you look just like the scum you are. The next time I see you, I want you to look like Soviet soldiers. I want your boots to be as shiny as the balls of a cat. . . ." In ever more curdling language the abasement and intimidation continued until Belenko concluded the man was serious, that all this was real.

Well, millions of others have been in the same situation. It's bound to be better when we start flying.

They would not fly, however, for a long while. After completing basic military training, the standard Course for Young Warriors administered to all recruits, the cadets were transferred to an air base on the other side of Armavir. There they began fifteen months of academic studies: science of communism, history of the Party, Marxist/Leninist philosophy, mathematics, physics, electronics, tactics, navigation, topography, military regulations, and aerodynamics. Classes started at 7:30 A.M., after breakfast and inspection, and continued until 7:30 P.M. six days a week. On Sunday morning they swabbed, swept, or dusted all crannies of the barracks; then a political officer treated them to a two-hour dissertation about current world events.

A television crew preparing a special program about flight training at Armavir filmed the cadets as they took state examinations in September. A couple of days afterward Belenko was summoned to the office of the commandant and informed that because of his handsome appearance and because he ranked first on the exams, he had been designated to appear on the program. A commentator interviewed him before the cameras, and he became something of a celebrity after the program was shown on Armavir television.

The cadets received their first leave in September and vouchers enabling them to fly via Aeroflot anywhere in the Soviet Union for a few rubles. Various friends invited Belenko to stay with their families in Moscow, Leningrad, and Kirov. But a feeling of obligation or the yearning for a sense of family he never had had or a vague hope that things might be different impelled him to visit Rubtsovsk.

He appeared in a new blue uniform with the gold, black, and blue shoulder boards of a cadet, emblems denoting that he was, as he looked, a special soldier picked and destined by his country to be much more. The pride he thought he saw in his father's face momentarily made him proud, and his stepmother fawned over him. They were impressed, and wanting their acquaintances to be impressed, they gave a party ostensibly in his honor. His father's wartime friend, the truck factory manager, a Party underling assigned to the factory, and a couple of others from the plant were invited. Belenko realized that all were people who might help the family in the future, that the party really was not for him. He did not blame them. He felt only embarrassment at the irreducible emotional distance apparent between him and his father and stepmother whenever they were alone. They had nothing meaningful to say to each other. They did not know each other; they never had and never would. Politely lying about his schedule, he moved out on the third day and looked up friends from high school.

One of his schoolmates had been killed in an automobile accident, and another imprisoned for black marketeering. Two had escaped to Moscow, one was in medical school, and another studying engineering. Most were working in factories, mainly the truck factory. The approbation his uniform and status evoked saddened, rather than heartened, him as he contrasted the richness of his future with the desolation of theirs.

The First Escape   *61*

In Omsk, Belenko sought out his best DOSAAF friend, Yuri Nikolayevich Sukhanov, who had grown up pretty much like him, largely forsaken by divorced parents. He remembered him as a tall, broad-shouldered boxer good enough to try out for the 1968 Olympics team, a free-spirited hell raiser, and one of the most promising flight students.

Now the sight of him appalled Belenko. He had gained twenty-five pounds, looked fifteen years older, and seemed sapped of all his characteristic vibrance. Nevertheless, he insisted that Belenko share a bottle of vodka in his room, and the entreaties were so earnest Belenko had to accede.

An injury Sukhanov sustained in boxing had permanently impaired his vision, precluding him from passing Air Force physicals and from fighting anymore. He had married a wonderful girl, a secretary at the electronics plant where he worked, and had tried to study electronic engineering at night school. But with the birth of their baby, the combined pressures of work, study, and family overwhelmed him, and he dropped out of school. They could find time for little other than what daily subsistence required. Sometimes food shopping alone, which they could undertake only before or after work, consumed two to three hours because they had to line up at different stores for bread, vegetables, staples, and meat.

Sukhanov's wife, Irina, was sitting on the bed nursing the baby when they entered. Belenko judged the room was about nine yards long and three yards wide. The bed, a crib, a small desk, one chair, and the cupboard and refrigerator took up most of the space. There was a small communal kitchen at the end of the hall; the toilet was in an outhouse. Irina welcomed Belenko as graciously as the circumstances allowed, putting the baby in the crib and setting out bread and canned fish on the desk, which also served as a dining table. Half-consciously, Belenko, in recounting life in flight school, tried to emphasize the negative—the petty tyrannies, hardships and restrictions and seeming stupidities of military life. Sukhanov finally stopped him. "Thank you, Viktor. But I would give anything to be in your place."

Raucous shouts greeted Belenko at Factory 13, and a crowd of workers formed around him. "Send out for juice!" But Belenko produced the vodka, making himself all the more of a hero. He questioned them, hunting for evidence of change, of some improvement. There was none. It was the same except that in his eyes the swamp now was more fearful than ever. For once, he drank with them without restraint and for the same reason, but no amount of alcohol could blur or alter what he saw.

There was alarm at Armavir when Belenko returned from leave. A cholera epidemic had spread from the shores of the Black Sea through the region, and all military personnel were being quarantined indefinitely on their bases. A military physician briefed the cadets about the nature and dangers of cholera, noting that one good antidote was "vodka with garlic." Belenko was astounded, for from his own reading, he already knew about cholera.

Cholera! If we have the best medicine in the world, why should we have cholera? Cholera is a disease of the yellows and blacks. It is a disease of filth. Well, of course. There is shit and filth and garbage everywhere: on the beaches, in the outhouse and garbage pit of every house, every apartment building. People can't bathe or even wash their dishes properly. What can you expect? How many toilets could we build for the price of one spaceship?

The cholera epidemic was followed by an outbreak of a virulent and infectious respiratory ailment, then by an epidemic of hoof-and-mouth disease. In consequence, the cadets were locked on base throughout the autumn and winter. The knowledge that he could not look forward to even a few hours of freedom had a claustrophobic effect on Belenko and may have contributed to his brooding. Regardless, he experienced a resurgence of intellectual conflict and corrosive doubts. The political officers, to make their points intelligible, had to disclose some facts, and Belenko's analysis of these facts plunged him into ever-deepening spiritual trouble.

To demonstrate the inherent injustice and totalitarian

nature of American society, a political officer declared that the Communist Party was terribly persecuted in the United States. *Wait a minute! You mean they have a Communist Party in the United States; they allow it? Why, that would be like our allowing a Capitalist Party in the Soviet Union!*

To illustrate the persecution of the Communist Party, political instructors dwelt on the case of Angela Davis, a black and an avowed communist, once dismissed from the faculty of the University of California on grounds of incompetence. She was subsequently arrested but ultimately acquitted of murder—conspiracy charges arising from the killing of a California judge abducted in the midst of a trial.

You mean the Americans allow communists to teach in their universities? Why did the Dark Forces let her go? Why didn't they just kill her?

To prove that the American masses were basically sympathetic to communism and opposed to the imperialistic policies of the Dark Forces that held them underfoot, the political officers showed films of some of the great antiwar demonstrations.

You mean that in America you can just go out and demonstrate and raise hell and tear up things if you don't like something! Why, what would happen here if people rioted to protest our sending soldiers to Czechoslovakia? Well, we know what would happen.

To dramatize the poverty, hunger, and unemployment of contemporary America, the political officers showed films taken in the 1930s of Depression breadlines, current Soviet television films of New York slums and of workers eating sandwiches or hot dogs and drinking Coca-Cola for lunch. The narrative, explaining that a sandwich or hot dog was all the American could afford for "dinner," struck Belenko because in the Soviet Union the noon meal is the main one of the day.

If they are starving and can't find jobs and prefer communism, why don't they come over here? We need workers, millions of them, especially in Siberia, and we could guarantee them all the bread they need and milk, too. But wait a minute. Who owns all those cars I see?

In a spirit of logical inquiry, Belenko asked about the cars visible everywhere in the films. The instructor commended him for the prescience of his question and answered it with relish. True, the Dark Forces permitted many workers to have cars and houses as well; not only that, they also had built highways all across the land. But they charged the workers tolls to travel the highways, and they made the worker mortgage his whole life for the car and house. If he lost his job or got sick, he was ruined, wiped out, impoverished for life; he was a slave to the bankers and thus controlled by the Dark Forces.

That's very clever of the Dark Forces. But . . . if I had to choose between having a car and a house now and maybe being wiped out later or waiting maybe fifteen years for an apartment, which would I choose?

The West and especially the United States were depicted as being in the throes of death. The forces of socialism, led by "our Mother Country," were advancing everywhere—in the Middle East, Africa, Latin America, and Cuba (referred to as "our aircraft carrier"). The Americans no longer were all-powerful. To see their deterioration, one had only to look at their internal strife and the irresolute flaccidity they displayed in Vietnam.

Yet no week passed without warnings of the dreadful threat posed by the encircling Dark Forces of the West and their plots "to kidnap our Mother Country." This ubiquitous threat justified every sacrifice of material and human resources necessary to build Soviet armed forces into the mightiest in the world.

If they are so weak, why are they such a threat? What is the truth?

In tactics, the cadets studied mostly the methods of the Americans, the Main Enemy, whom they primarily were being trained to confront. A professor who had flown MiGs in Korea and served as an adviser to the North Vietnamese was frank in his characterization of U.S. pilots. They were professionally skilled and personally brave. Even when ambushed by larger numbers of MiGs jumping up at them from sanctuaries in China, they would stay and fight rather than flee. They drove on toward their targets no matter how many missiles, how much flak was fired at them. The Americans were quick and flexible in adapting to new situations or weapons, and they were ingenious in innovating surprises of their own. You never could be sure of what to expect from them except they always loved to fight.

The students asked a number of questions, as they were encouraged to do, and one wanted to know why the Americans were so good.

The professor explained that over the years they had perfected an extremely effective training program. They had developed psychological tests that enabled them to identify candidates with the highest aptitudes for flying and combat. Their recruits already had attended universities and thus began training with a "strong theoretical base." And virtually all their instructors had a great deal of actual combat experience because the Americans always were fighting somewhere in the world.

Yes, but how can such a rotten and decadent society produce pilots so brave?

A political officer supplied the answer. "Oh, they do it for money. They are extraordinarily well paid. They will do anything for money."

I wonder how much they pay them to make them willing to die.

His analysis of the case of the My Lai massacre in Vietnam probably disturbed Belenko most of all. Political officers proclaimed the slaughter of more than a hundred Vietnamese men, women, and children at the village of My Lai the ultimate example of American inhumanity and degeneracy. To demonstrate that the mass murder had actually occurred, they quoted verbatim from numerous American press accounts reporting the atrocity in macabre detail. There could be no doubt about it. The Americans themselves publicly had charged one of their own officers with the killing of 109 innocent civilians.*

But why are the Dark Forces putting him in jail? If they are pure and true Dark Forces, he did just what they wanted. They should be giving him a medal. And why do the Dark Forces allow their newspapers to tell about all this? Every society has its animals. I myself have seen some of ours in Rubtsovsk. Our newspapers won't even report one murder. But the Americans are shaming themselves in front of the whole world by reporting the murder of one hundred nine men, women and babies. Why?

His disquietude, however, receded before the prospect of flight. Belenko and some ninety other cadets were transferred to an air base eight miles outside Grozny near the Caspian Sea. Grozny was an ancient city of nearly 400,000, and undoubtedly it once had been lovely. The baroque architecture, ornate buildings, and cable cars gliding through narrow brick streets still made it somewhat attractive. But it stood in a valley which captured and held the smoke, pollutants, and stench discharged from surrounding oil refineries and chemical factories, and the river running through the city was an open sewer of industrial wastes.

At the base a KGB officer delivered an orientation lecture. After cautioning against Western spies, he spoke at length about the Chechens, one of some hundred ethnic and racial minorities that constitute the Soviet population. Native inhabitants of the eastern Caucasus, the Chechens were fiercely independent Muslims, racially akin to Iranians, who never had been satisfactorily subjugated by the czars or communists. Fearing that out of their hatred for Russians they would collaborate with the Germans, Stalin had deported them en masse to Kazakhstan. Cast into cold deserts and infertile mountains, they had suffered privation and hunger and perished in vast numbers. Khrushchev had allowed the sur-

---

* Army Lt. William Calley was later convicted by a court-martial jury of the killing of 22 civilians.

vivors to go back to their native region around Grozny. When they returned, they found their land, homes, shops, and jobs had been appropriated by Russians. Convinced of their righteousness, they commenced to kill Russians indiscriminately and barbarically, usually with knives. A young Russian sailor coming home from five years at sea was slashed to death in the railway station before his terror-stricken mother in 1959. Russian residents thereupon formed vigilante groups armed with axes, took out after the Chechens, then stormed government offices, demanding intervention to protect them from the wild Muslims. Troops, backed by tanks and armored cars, had to be called in to restore civil order. The government warned the Chechens that if they persisted in cutting up Russians, they all would be "sent far north where the polar bears live." The wholesale butchery largely subsided, but not individual murders, and many Chechen youths still subscribed to the credo that true manhood could not be attained without the killing of at least one Russian.

"Most of all, you must guard yourself against the Chechens," the KGB officer said. "The Chechens use knives wantonly, and under stress they will butcher you. You know how valuable you are to our country. It is your patriotic duty to take care and ensure your own safety. Never sleep on duty. Always stand watch with a long knife."

It sounds like hell around here! They will just butcher you for nothing! It sounds like we're in the darkest of Africa in the last century, like an outpost among savages. But this is 1969! The Soviet Union! And the Party says we've solved the nationality problem.

Flight instructor Grigori Petrovich Litvinov, tall, thin, and prematurely bald at thirty-one, looked and acted like an ascetic, abstaining totally from alcohol, tobacco, and profanity. He wore about him an air of perpetual calm and, in Belenko's hearing, never raised his voice. Upon being introduced, he insisted that they address each other by first names and admonished Belenko not to fear asking questions, however naïve. "I will answer the same question a hundred times,

I will stay up all night with you if need be, until you understand."

There was no need for such special attention. After being familiarized with the L-29 jet trainer, Belenko managed it more easily and surely than he had the old prop plane in which he had learned. The wasteful, melancholy waiting in Omsk, the submission to the straitjacket life of a cadet were now repaid by his certainty that he had done right. Alone in the cockpit, he was serenely free and unbound; he was where he knew he belonged.

Toward the end of the six months of basic flight training at Grozny, Litvinov and Belenko were changing clothes in the locker room. As Litvinov picked up his flight suit to hang it in the locker, a thick little book, small enough to be hidden behind a man's palm, tumbled out of a front flap pocket onto the floor. Belenko glanced down and saw the title of the book: Holy Bible. Litvinov's eyes were waiting to meet his when he looked up. They asked: Will you inform? Belenko's answered: Never.

Neither said anything, nor was the incident ever mentioned subsequently. Belenko thought about it, though. *It's his business what he reads. If the Bible is full of myths and fairy tales, let everybody see that for himself. Everybody knows that a lot of what the Party makes us read is full of shit; we can see and prove that for ourselves. Why not let everybody read anything he wants to? We know our system is the best. Why be afraid of other ideas when we can show they are not as good? Unless . . . unless, of course, we're afraid that our ideas aren't the best.*

The schedule stipulated that the cadets would study the MiG-17 for two months back at Armavir preparatory to the final phase of training. But the two months stretched into four because an emergency had sprung up in the countryside—another harvest was nearing. Each weekend and sometimes two or three more days a week, officers and men alike were packed into buses and trucks to join the battle of the harvest. For Belenko, it was a pleasant diversion. They mostly picked fruit and ate all they wanted. Because the schools and colleges of Armavir had been closed for the harvest, many pretty girls worked and flirted with them in the orchards. The farmers were hospitable and slipped them glasses of cider and wine. And at night they went back to the barracks, a good meal, and a clean bunk.

Yet Belenko despaired at the acres and acres of apples, tens of thousands, maybe hundreds of thousands of apples, rotting because nobody had arranged for them to be picked in time. He remembered how precious apples were in Siberia, how once in Rubtsovsk he had paid a whole ruble to buy one apple on the black market.

Why doesn't anything work? Why doesn't anything change? It's barely ten years before 1980. But we're no farther along toward True Communism than we were when they first started talking about it. We're never going to have True Communism. Everything is just as screwed up as ever. Why?

In April 1970 Belenko was assigned to a MiG-17 training regiment seventy-five miles northwest of Armavir near Tikhoretsk, whose 40,000 residents worked mainly in canneries and wineries. Although not accorded the privileges of officers, the cadets now, by and large, were treated as full-fledged pilots. They arose at 4:00 A.M. for a bountiful breakfast, then flew two or three times, breaking for a second breakfast around 9:30. The main meal at noon, which always included meat and fruit, was followed by a nap of an hour or so. They attended classes from early afternoon until early evening— tactics, future trends in aerodynamics, technology of advanced aircraft, military leadership, political economics, science of communism, history of the Party, Marxist/Leninist philosophy. Passes were issued on Saturday nights and Sundays, unless they were called to clean factories or work in the fields on weekends, requests which occurred roughly every other week.

Fortune again gave Belenko a good flight instructor, Lieutenant Nikolai Igoryevich Shvartzov, who was only twenty-four. He longed to be a test pilot and was able enough; but he had given up this ambition because he had no influence in Moscow, and nobody, so it was believed, could become a test pilot without influence. At the outset, Shvartzov gave Belenko only two instructions: "Let's be completely honest with each other about everything; that way we can trust and help each other," and, "If a MiG-17 ever goes into a spin, eject at once. You can pull it out of a spin, but it's hard. We can always build another plane. We can't build another you." Throughout their relationship, they were honest and got along well.

The MiG-17, light, swift, maneuverable, was fun to fly, and Belenko had confidence in it. Vietnam had proven that, if skillfully flown at lower altitudes, it could cope with the American F-4 Phantom. Should he duel with an American pilot in an F-4, the outcome would depend on which of them was the braver and better pilot. It would be a fair fight. That was all he asked.

Every four or five weeks the regiment received a secret intelligence bulletin reporting developments in American air power—characteristics, strengths, weaknesses, numbers to be manufactured, where and for which purposes they would be deployed. The bulletins were exceedingly factual and objective, devoid of comment or opinion and dryly written.

Reading quickly, as was his habit, Belenko scanned a description of the new F-14 fighter planned for the U.S. Navy and started another section before the import of what he had read struck him. "What?" he exclaimed aloud. "What did I read?" He reread the data about the F-14. It would be equipped with radar that could detect aircraft 180 miles away, enable its fire-control system to lock onto multiple targets 100 miles away, and simultaneously fire six missiles that could hit six different aircraft eighty miles away—this even though the F-14 and hostile aircraft might be closing upon each other at a speed up to four times that of sound.

Our radar, when it works, has a range of fifty miles. Our missiles, when they work, have a range of eighteen miles. How will we fight the F-14? It will kill us before we ever see it!

Belenko put the question frankly to an aerodynamics pro-

fessor the next afternoon. The professor stammered, equivo-
cated, evaded. Every aircraft has certain weaknesses. It is
only a question of uncovering them and learning how to
exploit them. It may be possible to attack the F-14 from close
range with superior numbers.

*Shit. That's ridiculous. Besides, if what our own intelligence
says is true, the F-14 still could outfly anything we have even if
we got close to it.*

The professor who taught the technology of advanced aircraft was respected for his intelligence and technical background, so Belenko asked him openly in class. He answered
succinctly. We presently have nothing to equal the F-14. We
are experimenting with something that could be the answer.
It is designated Product 84.

Subsequently Belenko read details of the F-15 being built
as an air-superiority fighter for the U.S. Air Force, then accounts of the planned B-1 bomber, and they were still more
devastating to him. The F-15 would fly at nearly three times
the speed of sound and climb to altitudes above 60,000 feet
faster than any plane in the world, and at very low levels,
where metallurgical problems restricted the speed of Soviet
fighters, it could hopelessly outdistance anything the Russians had. The capabilities of the B-1 seemed other-worldly. A
thousand miles away from the Soviet Union, it could com-
mence firing missiles armed with decoys and devices to nul-
lify radar and nuclear weapons to shatter defenses. Then it
could drop to tree-top level, beneath the reach of radar and
missiles, and, at speeds making it impervious to pursuit, skim
over the target area. Having unleashed a barrage of nuclear
bombs, it could skyrocket away at extreme altitudes, at 1400
miles an hour.

The professor of technology again was candid. He said
that presently there was no known defense, practical or theoretical, against the B-1 should it perform approximately as
designed. The history of warfare demonstrated that for every
offensive weapon, an effective defensive weapon ultimately
emerged, and doubtless, one would be developed. The

broader difficulty lay in Soviet technological deficiencies. The Russians still could not develop an aircraft engine that for the same weight generated the same thrust as an American engine. They were behind in electronics, transistors, and microcircuitry. And all technological difficulties were compounded by the comparative inadequacy of their computer technology. Cadets should not be discouraged by these handicaps but rather consider them a further stimulus to becoming better pilots than the Americans.

But if our system is so much better than the Americans', *why is their technology so much better than ours?*

Again, though, the thrill of flight, the excitement of personal success diverted him from the concern and skepticism such questions inspired. In July 1971 he passed his final flight examinations, receiving both the highest grade of five and a commendation. The 258 cadets remaining from the original class of 360 were ordered back to Armavir to study for the state examinations. But Belenko knew these were meaningless. It was over. Having brought them this far, the Party did not intend to lose any of them. He had done it. For more than four years he had done all the military, the Party, the Mother Country demanded. He had done it on his own, despite the oppressions, brutalities, risks, and stresses of cadet life, despite multiplying, heretical doubts about the Party he was sworn to serve. He was about to be what since boyhood he had aspired to be. And he was proud of himself.

The professors now tacitly treated the cadets as officers, and Belenko for the first time learned of all the benefits and perquisites bestowed on a Soviet pilot. To him they were breathtaking.

Whereas the average Soviet doctor or scientist was paid 120 to 130 rubles a month, and an educator only about 100, he would earn 300. The typical young Soviet couple waited seven to eight years, and often much longer, for an apartment, and the majority of Soviet dwellings still were without indoor plumbing. As a pilot Belenko was guaranteed an apartment with bath and kitchen, wherever stationed. Food constituted the largest item in most Soviet family budgets; meat and fresh vegetables frequently were unavailable; shopping was arduous and time-consuming. Pilots, wherever based, were entitled to four excellent free meals a day seven days a week. Ordinary citizens were allowed two weeks of vacation; pilots, forty-five days. Additionally, during vacation, pilots could fly anywhere in the Soviet Union on Aeroflot for a nominal fee. Normally a Soviet citizen did not retire before sixty-five; Belenko could retire at forty, receiving two-thirds of his regular salary for the rest of his life. There was more—the best medical care, free uniforms and shoes, little preferential privileges, and enormous prestige.

Belenko had known of some of these benefits. But their full range was kept secret, never published or discussed. *No wonder! If people knew how much more we get, they would detest us instead of liking us.*

A political officer at Armavir spoke to them about marriage, and though well intentioned, his advice was somewhat contradictory. He explained that because of the status and glamor of pilots, many girls were eager to marry them. Quite a few enrolled in school or took jobs in Armavir for that express purpose. While most were wholesome, a few were prostitutes. No one should enter into marriage quickly or lightly, because the effects of marriage would endure throughout life.

At the same time, though, the political officer emphasized the personal and professional advantages of marriage. It represented a healthy and natural form of life. Married pilots could awaken fresh in the morning, ready to fly, whereas bachelors were likely to dissipate themselves by prowling around bars, looking for women.

For reasons probably having little to do with the lectures, most cadets did marry shortly before or after graduation, and in late August Belenko attended one of the weddings. At the party afterward the bride introduced him to a twenty-year-old nursing student, Ludmilla Petrovna. She was blond, pretty, sensuous, and, to Belenko, ideal. Their physical attraction to each other was instant and mutual.

Their backgrounds, however, were dissimilar. Ludmilla was the only child of wealthy parents living in Magadan in the far northeast. Her father managed a large factory, her mother ran a brewery, and both had high Party connections in Moscow. She had never worked or wanted for anything and was accustomed to restaurants, to theaters, and to spending money as she pleased. Her parents had lavished clothes and jewelry on her, often taken her to Moscow and Leningrad and to special spas reserved for the well-connected. She shared none of his interests in literature, athletics, or the romance of flying. But the sexual magnetism between them was powerful and delightful, and even though they had seen each other only seven or eight times, they married after he was commissioned in October.

Belenko never had thought of himself as other than a fighter pilot. He expected to join a MiG-17 squadron, from which he hoped to graduate to MiG-23s or even MiG-25s, which continued to be cited as the most promising counter to the new generation of American fighters being deployed in the 1970s. When the Party commission released the assignments of the new officers, he ran to the office of the commandant to protest and appeal. He had been appointed a MiG-17 instructor—to him, the worst duty conceivable. He would be doing, albeit in a reverse role, the same thing he had been doing for the past two years. There would be no opportunity to improve professionally by flying more advanced aircraft, no excitement, no adventure.

"You have been honored, and you should feel honored," the commandant said. "The Party commission chose the best to be instructors."

"But I do not want to be an instructor."

"What kind of bordello would we have around here if everybody did only what he wants to do? You must serve where the Party decides you are needed, and I assure you we need instructors."

The December night was black, cold, and drenched with pelting rain, and when Belenko stepped on the train at 8:00

P.M., his mood matched the weather. He had been there before, twice, actually: on the train that had taken him from the Donbas to Rubtsovsk in 1953, and the train that had brought him from Omsk to Armavir in 1967. Everything was the same—the close, putrid air, the high wooden seats, the reeking toilet, the lack of beer or any amenities, the foul, unrelenting stink. His first duty station, Salsk, a city of 60,000, was only 100 or so miles away, but the train stopped frequently and did not arrive until 2:00 A.M.

The rain was still falling hard as he waded and slogged through muddy streets to the city's only hotel. It was full and locked for the night, and at that hour there was no transportation to the base five miles away, so he waded back to the station. All benches and virtually every square inch of the station floor were occupied by human bodies—*kolkhozniks* who had come to buy bread, salt, and soap; vagabonds and beggars in rags; dirty children, some with ugly red sores, others with pocked faces resembling old potatoes—all trying to sleep on newspapers, using their canvas boots or little shoes as pillows. The odor was almost as bad as on the train. There being no place to sit, he nudged out enough space to stand through the night, leaning against a post.

I wish they could see this, smell it, all of them, the whole Politburo, all those lying bastards who tell us every day and make us say every day how wonderful our progress is, how well-off and happy we are, how perfect everything will be by 1980. Look at these New Communist Men our society has produced! I would make them sit near the toilet so they could smell what is creeping out under the door. I would make them hold those children in their arms and look at those sores and then make speeches about the science of communism. Liars! Filthy liars!

At daylight a policeman halted a six-wheel truck able to negotiate the mud and induced the driver to deliver Lieutenant Belenko to his first post. His new uniform and boots were soiled and splattered with mud. In his thoughts, much more was indelibly soiled.

Nevertheless, Belenko shared the elation of all the other

newly arrived officers when they were handed keys to their apartments in a building that had been completed and certified for occupancy only a month before. To be promised an apartment was one thing; to be given an apartment as promised, quite another. Eagerly and expectantly Belenko unlocked the door and smelled dampness. The floor, built with green lumber, already was warped and wavy. Plaster was peeling off the walls. The windowpane in the kitchen was broken, and no water poured from the faucet. The bathtub leaked; the toilet did not flush. None of the electrical outlets worked.

Already gathered in the halls were other officers, who had found comparable conditions in their apartments. Together they marched forth to collar the construction superintendent responsible for building the apartments. Unmoved by their recitation of ills, he told them that the building had been inspected and approved by an acceptance commission from their regiment. Any deficiencies that might have developed subsequently were none of his concern.

This is outrageous. The Party must know. The Party must correct this.

Belenko and another lieutenant confronted the first Party representative they could find, a young political officer quartered in the same building. He was cynical, yet truthful. The building had not been inspected. The military builders sold substantial quantities of allotted materials on the black market, then bribed the chairman of the regimental acceptance commission and took the whole commission to dinner. There the acceptance papers were drunkenly signed without any commission member's ever having been inside the building. What was done could not now be undone.

During the day Belenko studied pedagogy, psychology, methodology of flight instruction, and political education in the course for instructors, and on weekends he visited Ludmilla in Armavir. At night he mastered the building trade. He relaid the floor, replastered the walls, calked the bathtub, repaired the toilet, replaced the faucets, and rewired the electrical sockets. He procured all the materials easily enough, not from stores, of course, but from the construction superintendent in exchange for vodka. By late February he had redone the whole interior rather handsomely.

Then one night he was awakened by a loud boom followed by crunching noises. The building was splitting. A seam about a foot wide opened from the living room out into the world, and a much more gaping one exposed his bedroom to his neighbor's living room. Huge cranes, trucks, and an army of workers were marshaled to save the building. They trussed and wrapped it in steel belts as if staving a barrel and inserted steel beams through the interior to keep it intact. The beam running through Belenko's living room looked odd, but he found it useful for chinning and other exercises.

The emergency measures proved effective for a while. But after three weeks or so the center of the building started to sag and kept sagging until the whole edifice assumed the configuration of a canoe.

It's an architectural marvel!

Still, the ceilings in his apartment drooped only a foot or two, and it was home, a private, unshared home, and he was intent on furnishing it as commodiously as possible for Ludmilla before she joined him in the spring after her graduation. Living alone and dining at the base, he had few expenses, and by March he had accumulated about 1,500 rubles, counting the 600 given him at commissioning. He bought a television for 450, a refrigerator for 300, and, for 250, a sofa that converted into a bed. The rest he conserved for a delayed wedding trip to Leningrad in April and to enable Ludmilla to pick furnishings of her choice.

One of the lieutenant colonels teaching the course for instructors was an irreverent cynic, marking time until his fortieth birthday and retirement, and he liked to regale the young lieutenants with caustic sayings about life in the Soviet military. Three of them were to recur often to Belenko.

To succeed in the Soviet Army, you must learn from the dog. You must know when and where to bark and when and where to lick.

A Soviet pilot without a pencil is like a man without a prick, for the mission of a Soviet pilot is to create paperwork. The more paper you have, the better to cover your ass.

Two close boyhood friends met for the first time since their graduation from the military academy twenty years before. One was a captain; the other, a general. "Why are you a general and I only a captain?"

"I will show you," replied the general, picking up a rock, holding it to his ear, and then handing it to the captain. "Listen to the noise the rock makes."

The captain listened and threw the rock away. "No, it makes no noise at all."

"You see, that is why you are still a captain. A general told you a rock makes noise, and you said no to a general."

To protect himself, the lieutenant colonel always emphasized with mock seriousness that such sayings represented misconceptions. Belenko was to learn, though, that each originated in reality.

After he commenced his duties as an instructor, the Party decided to expand and accelerate pilot training without, however, increasing the number of personnel and aircraft allocated for training. Previously one instructor had at his disposal two MiG-17s, two flight engineers, and four enlisted mechanics to teach three students. But with the same resources Belenko had to teach six students, and in good weather he flew incessantly, taking them up successively throughout the day. Flying still was fun, although not as much fun as when he flew alone. After the fortieth or fiftieth loop of the day, a loop was not so interesting.

The serious problems all occurred on the ground. Belenko did not just supervise the twelve men under him. He was held personally accountable for their behavior twenty-four hours a day. He was supposed to regulate, record, and report their every action and, insofar as possible, their every thought, to know and watch every detail of their lives, including the most intimate and personal details. And he had to draft and be prepared to exhibit for inspection by political officers at any time a written program specifying precisely what he was doing daily to develop each of his subordinates into a New Communist Man.

Having landed for the ninth time on a day that had begun at 4:00 A.M., Belenko was exhausted. Dusk was settling, and a light drizzle starting to fall, when a messenger—there were no telephones—delivered a summons from the political officer.

"So, Comrade Lieutenant, we see that you do not know your men; you do not know how to educate them."

"I do not understand, Comrade."

"Read this, and you will understand." The KGB had uncovered a letter written by one of Belenko's mechanics, a twenty-year-old private, to his parents. The soldier recited his miseries—the sparse, repulsive rations, the congested barracks, the practice through which second-year soldiers extorted food from first-year soldiers by pouncing upon the recalcitrants during the night, covering them with blankets, and beating them mercilessly.

"Do you see what a dark shadow such a letter throws over our Army?"

"But, Comrade, look at the date. The letter was written ten months ago, long before I was here."

The point was unarguable, and the political officer was flustered, but not for long. "Let me see your program for this man."

Belenko handed over the notebook he always was required to keep with him. "Your failure is clear. There is not one mention here of the works of Leonid Ilyich [Brezhnev]. How can your mechanic develop politically without knowledge of the thoughts of the Party's leader? You see, Comrade Lieutenant, you have not worked very productively today."

You pig, I ought to smash in your fat face. I flew my ass off today, flew all to hell and back. I did one hundred rolls, sixty dead loops, sixty Immelmanns. What do you know about work? I'd like to put you to work in an aircraft. You'd puke and fill your pants in one minute.

"Comrade, I see my mistake. I will try to do better."

Belenko repeatedly was upbraided because of the behavior of one of his flight engineers, who was an alcoholic. He stole, drank, and sometimes sold the alcohol stored in copious quantities for the coolant and braking systems of the MiG-17. Now everybody in the regiment—the commander, the officers, the men, Belenko himself—at times drank this alcohol. Not only was it available and free, but because the alcohol was produced for aircraft, it was more purely distilled than the standard vodka produced for the people. In fact, the aircraft alcohol was so valued on the black market that in the regiment it was called white gold. The trouble was that the flight engineer drank so much and continuously that he staggered around all day, frequently making a spectacle of himself and, as Belenko's superiors stressed, setting an "improper example."

Belenko talked several times to the engineer, who was sixteen years older than he and had been in the service twenty-two years. He reasoned, he pleaded, he threatened, he appealed, all to no avail, because the man in his condition could no more stop drinking than he could stop breathing.

Finally, Belenko was rebuked for "leadership failure." In response he wrote a formal report recommending that the engineer either be provided with psychiatric treatment or be dismissed from the service. The next morning a deputy regimental commander called Belenko in and told him that if he would withdraw the report, his reprimand would also be withdrawn, and the flight engineer transferred. Amazed, Belenko shrugged and complied.

Training standards inevitably suffered under the intensified pressures to graduate more pilots. In his training Belenko had flown 300 hours—100 in the L-29, 200 in the MiG-17—and these had been "honest" hours—that is, they actually were flown. Now cadets were flying only 200 hours, and not all these were "honest." There also was a slight slippage in the quality of pilot candidates, and although five of Belenko's students were able, the sixth was beyond salvage. He simply lacked the native ability to fly. Belenko dared not allow him to solo in a MiG-17, and whenever he entrusted him with the controls, the results were frightening. Though he personally liked the cadet, Belenko formally recommended his dismissal. Another uproar and demand that he rescind the recommendation ensued. But this time Belenko in conscience could not accede. Aloft, the cadet was a menace to everybody and to himself. Even if he learned to take off and land, he never could do much else except fly in circles, and his every flight would be a potential disaster. Thus, the issue and Belenko ultimately were brought before the regimental commander, who also tried to induce retraction of the report. Failing, the commander announced that he himself would fly with the cadet and pronounce his own judgment. Most likely he intended to overrule Belenko, but he was sufficiently shaken upon landing to concur, reluctantly, that dismissal was the only option.

Belenko spent the better part of a month completing the mountains of paperwork requisite to dismissal. In the process he finally comprehended why no one in his own class had been expelled, why second-year soldiers who preyed on neophytes were not prosecuted, why the flight engineer was not cashiered, why the cadet would not have been dismissed had he not been egregiously hopeless.

The Party had decreed that a certain number of qualified pilots would be trained in a given time. The Party had decreed that pilots, officers, soldiers, all would be transformed into New Communist Men. That was the plan. A commander who publicly disciplined a subordinate or dismissed a student risked the wrath and punishment of the Party by convicting himself, *ipso facto*, of incompetence, of undermining the plan.

The consequent fear created a system in which problems were masked and perpetuated, rather than eliminated, and it spawned corruption or a psychological environment in which corruption flourished. Prior to an inspection by senior officers of the Air Defense Command, Belenko was scheduled to perform a complicated one-hour exercise in which he and a student in another MiG would intercept and down a third MiG. The exercise would be recorded on the films of gun cameras and chronometer tapes for examination by the inspectors. But the morning of the planned exercise, the sky was filled with thunder and lightning.

Nevertheless, a deputy regimental commander ordered them to fly. "What! That's impossible."

"Listen to me. Just tell your student to climb up to five hundred meters. You make a quick intercept, and both of you come right back down. It won't take five minutes. I'll show you how to fix it when you get back."

For the next three days Belenko and the deputy commander juggled films and tapes to fabricate a record of an elaborate and successful exercise. When they finished, one obstacle remained. What about the fuel? They had flown six minutes. The records showed the exercise had lasted sixty minutes. How to explain the leftover fuel? Dump it. So thousands of gallons of jet fuel were dumped on the ground.

On a typical flying day, Belenko arose at 3:30 A.M. to catch the bus that left at 4:00 for the base, where he had breakfast, underwent a medical examination, and briefed his students prior to the first takeoff at 7:00. He flew with them until 1:00 P.M., when the main meal of the day was served. From 2:00 to 3:00 P.M. he and his fellow instructors customarily were berated by the training squadron commander and a political officer for the failures, on and off duty, of their students and subordinates. Unable to articulate or manifest his anger at the daily censure, he attended to paperwork and counseled students until supper at 6:00 P.M. Unless paperwork or political conferences detained him, he usually arrived home by bus around 7:30 P.M. To be fresh and alert by 3:00 the next day, he needed to go to sleep as quickly as possible.

On Sunday, his lone day off, he wanted and needed to rest. Ludmilla, who worked at a hospital six days a week, wanted to go out, to do something, and they argued about how the day should be spent. Ludmilla complained about much else.

She abhorred Salsk and the life of a military wife, and Belenko understood her feelings. Salsk, a place where "undesirables" had been sent in Czarist times, was a drab, dingy, poor city set on treeless flatlands over which stinging winds howled. Dust intruded everywhere except when rain turned it to mud. The two motion-picture theaters were small, and you rarely could enter without waiting more than an hour. Service in the city's few restaurants also meant more than an hour's wait and the fare was not worth the delay. There was no officers' club at the base, nor any other facility that wives might enjoy. Unable to change these circumstances or his working hours, which she also resented, Belenko could only sympathize and ask that she bear up in hope of eventual transfer to a more pleasant duty station.

Money was another and more disruptive source of conflict. Ludmilla earned 65 rubles a month as a nurse, and their combined income of 365 rubles was princely by Soviet standards. Unless he were to become a KGB officer or Party official, and either possibility was unthinkable, there was no pursuit that would pay him as much. But she nagged him for not earning more, and they often were short because she spent so capriciously and made costly trips to Magadan. At first he tried to indulge her.

Let life teach her. She is young and will grow.

On the chance that they could duplicate the happiness of their wedding trip, he proposed that during his next leave they vacation in Leningrad. About a week before they were to depart, he discovered that she had bought a ring for 140 rubles, spending most of the money he had saved for the trip. He vented his rage, and she announced her intention of divorcing him and returning to her parents.

He dissuaded her by reasoning that they simply were experiencing the kind of crisis that besets all young married couples, and soon she was pregnant. A child, he thought, would reunite them emotionally by giving them a new, shared interest. And for a while after the birth of their healthy son, Dmitri, in January 1973, they did share parental joy. But working twelve to fourteen hours daily six days a week, Belenko seldom could be with the child. The necessity of caring for him confined Ludmilla and thereby intensified her disdain of their mode of life. Instead of lessening their tensions, the baby exacerbated them. Their marriage deteriorated into sullen hostility, and disagreements over trivial issues erupted into acrimonious quarrels.

In their continuing efforts to inculcate pilots with the conviction that the United States symbolized the quintessence of degeneracy, political officers dwelt on the unfolding Watergate scandals. The details confused Belenko, and by now he was skeptical of anything the political officers said. But what he did understand at the culmination of the scandals heightened his skepticism. The President of the United States had been compelled to resign in disgrace, and other ranking figures of the American government faced prosecution and probable imprisonment, all because, so far as he could determine, they had lied.

You mean they can throw out their leader and put his men in jail just because they lied! Why, if we did that here, the whole Politburo and every Party official in the country would be in jail! Why, here, if you know somebody in the Party, you can do anything you want, you can kill a man, and you won't go to jail. I've seen that for myself.

And where are the Dark Forces? If the Dark Forces control everything in America and put their own men in power, why would they let their men be thrown out? The truth must be that the Dark Forces can't control everything. But if they don't control everything, then the Party is lying again. What does the Party tell the truth about?

Belenko seldom had cause or time to venture into downtown Salsk at night, but bachelor pilots did, and though they often were assaulted by robbers who knew they had money, they were under the strictest of orders never to engage in violence lest they injure themselves. The attacks proliferated, and one evening a gang of sadistic thugs killed an officer, blinded a second with sulfuric acid, and partially blinded a third as they emerged from a restaurant. Thereafter pilots were forbidden to enter Salsk after dark.

Sometimes Belenko did go into the city to shop for Ludmilla at the bazaar where on Sundays *kolkhozniks* sold poultry and produce from their plots. Beggars congregated at the open-air market, and some brought along emaciated children to heighten public pity; tramps crawled around the stalls like scavengers searching the ground for scraps of vegetables. Generally there was much to buy at the bazaar, but everything was expensive. A kilogram of potatoes or tomatoes cost one ruble; a small chicken, ten; a duck, twelve; a turkey, forty— one-third the monthly salary of the average doctor. In winter prices were much higher.

Each fall Belenko had to organize his twelve subordinates into a labor squad and sortie forth into the annual battle of the harvest. Treading through the dust or mud and manure of the *kolkhoz*, they reaped grain, tinkered with neglected machinery, and tried to toil usefully alongside the women, children, students, and old men. The sight of Air Force pilots, engineers, and mechanics so deployed made him alternately curse and laugh.

They brag all the time of our progress—in the newspaper, on radio, and television. Where is the progress? It's all the same: the crime, the poverty, the stupidity. We're never going to have a New Communist Man; we're never going to have True Communism.

Each squadron at the base had a Lenin Room, where pilots could watch Brezhnev's televised speeches and read *Pravda,* as they were required to do, and occasionally chat. After a Brezhnev speech, someone referred sarcastically to an exchange of letters between a worker and Brezhnev, published in *Pravda.* "Let's write him a letter about our shitty aircraft and ask him for some nice F-15s." Nobody talked that way except Lieutenant Nikolai Ivanovich Krotkov. There was no doubt that Krotkov was brilliant. He had graduated from flight school with a gold medal, played guitar and sang superbly, and could recite forbidden poetry verbatim by the hour. This was perilous. He had already been warned about singing the forbidden songs of Aleksandr Galich, the famous

Russian satirist who was expelled because of his ideological irreverence.

Shortly before supper three or four days later, Belenko and other instructors saw Krotkov acting as if he had gone mad. Furiously cursing, he was smashing his guitar to bits against a tree. When quieted, he told them he had just come from a confrontation with the KGB.

You have a big mouth, the KGB officer told him. If you keep opening it, we are going to kick you out of the service. Despite your gold medal, you will find no job; nobody will touch you. So, unless you want to starve, you had better stop singing dirty songs and reciting dirty poems. You had better zip up your mouth for good.

Belenko recalled a stanza from a patriotic Soviet march—"Where can man breathe so freely. . . ." *What kind of freedom do we have when we are afraid of a song or a poem?*

About the time of the Krotkov incident Belenko—who had been made an instructor for the SU-15 high-performance interceptor—heard a rumor. Supposedly a pilot had stolen an AN-2 transport and attempted to fly to Turkey. MiGs overtook and shot him down over the Black Sea.

If I were in an SU-15 and had enough fuel, nobody would ever catch me.

The thought was terrible, obscene; instantly and in shame he banished it, daring not entertain it a millisecond more. But the thought had occurred.

In the autumn of 1975 Belenko decided to request officially a transfer to a combat unit, preferably a MiG-25 squadron. The squadron commander, deputy regimental commander, and regimental commander all tried by a combination of cajolery and ridicule to dissuade him from "forsaking duty" or "acting like a test pilot." But the transfer request was submitted precisely as military regulations authorized, and each had no legal choice except to forward it until the matter reached the school commandant, Major General Dmitri Vasilyevich Golodnikov.

The general, a portly, bald man in his late fifties, sat behind a polished desk in his large office furnished with a long conference table covered by red velvet, a dozen chairs, red curtains, wall maps, and a magnificent Oriental rug. Belenko, who had never met a general, was surprised that he spoke so affably.

He understood, even admired Belenko's motives. He himself would prefer to be with combat forces in Germany or the Far East, where one might "see some action." But the overriding desire of every officer must be to serve the Party, and the Party needed him here. In a combat squadron he would provide the Party with one pilot; as an instructor he was providing the Party with many. Therefore, Golodnikov asked that Belenko withdraw his request, take some leave, and resume his duties with fresh dedication. If he had any problems, with his apartment or anything else, they could be worked out.

Belenko thanked the general but said that having been an instructor almost four years, he believed he could best serve the Party by becoming a more accomplished pilot, and that he could not do unless he learned to fly more sophisticated combat aircraft.

"Belenko, let's be frank with each other. You are an excellent instructor and a fine officer. Both your record and your superiors tell me that. You know as well as I that many of the young instructors they are sending us are not ready to be instructors; they barely can fly themselves. That is why we cannot afford to lose experienced instructors. I am not proposing that you spend the rest of your career as an instructor. I will be retiring in a couple of years, and I have friends. When I leave, I shall see that they help you."

Belenko understood the invitation to accept initiation into the system, to sell himself to the system. Yet it only reinforced his determination. When he said no a second time, Golodnikov abruptly dropped the mask of reason and affability.

"You are defying me!"

"No, sir, Comrade General. I am making a request in accordance with the regulations of the Soviet Army."

"Your request is denied."

"But, Comrade General, the regulations say that my request must be forwarded."

"That matter is closed."

"You will not forward my request?"

"You are dismissed. You may leave."

Belenko stood up and stared straight into the eyes of the general. "I have something to say."

"What?"

"I will stay in this school. I will work harder to follow every rule and regulation, to teach the students to fly, to enforce discipline in our regiment and school, to combat drunkenness, the theft of alcohol, the forgeries, embezzlement, and corruption that exist everywhere in our school. To do that, it will be necessary to dismiss from the Army certain officers and commanders who are aiding and abetting these practices. And to do *that*, it will be necessary for me to write a letter to the Minister of Defense, in accordance with the *Soviet Army Manual of Discipline*, proving what is going on in our school."

"You may not do that."

"Why not? It's strictly in accordance with regulations. Let me tell you some of the things I will say. I will talk first about the death of Lieutenant Lubach and his student. The investigating commission said it was an accident. It was murder. You said that many of our young instructors are not qualified. But why do you certify them as qualified? Why did you send Lieutenant Lubach's records to a combat squadron and have them returned so it would look as if he had experience in a combat squadron when you knew he couldn't fly? Why did you let him take that student up and kill himself and the student?"

The general's face flushed. "That is none of your business."

Belenko cited a colonel, one of the general's deputies, who, while piously haranguing officers to curb alcoholism, supervised the wholesale theft of aircraft alcohol, even using military trucks to transport it into Salsk for sale.

"All right. We know about that. That is being taken care of."

Next, Belenko detailed how officers forged records and reported more flight time than had been flown so as to obtain excesses of alcohol and how huge quantities of aviation fuel were being dumped to keep the records consistent.

"All right. What next? Go on."

Belenko recalled how during a recent practice alert another of Golodnikov's aides, a lieutenant colonel, had staggered among students on the flight line, raving incoherently, provoking laughter, and causing one student to say aloud, "To hell with all this. Let's go have a drink."

"That officer has been punished."

But Belenko sensed that his blows were telling, and he went on, reconstructing a suppressed scandal involving a colonel in charge of housing. The colonel kept a second apartment that was supposed to be allocated to an officer, and there employed prostitutes to entertain visiting dignitaries. A general from Moscow was so taken by one of these young ladies that he locked her in the apartment for three days and nights. It happened that the girl was, or at least the KGB believed her to be, a Western agent, and during one of those three nights she was scheduled to meet her clandestine supervisor, in whom the KGB was most interested. When she failed to appear, the other agent became alarmed and escaped. The KGB ascertained some of the truth, but Golodnikov or others concealed enough to allow the colonel to retire quietly without being punished and without calling down upon themselves the righteous vindictiveness of State Security.

Golodnikov, who had avoided Belenko's stare, now stared back at him with sheer hatred.

"There is more. . . ."

"Enough! Nothing you have said has anything to do with your duties as an instructor. This is pure blackmail." Golodnikov pressed a buzzer, and an aide appeared. "Tell the chief of the hospital to report to me immediately. Immediately! No matter what he is doing."

Belenko saluted and started to leave. "No, Belenko. You stay. You had your chance. Now it is too late for you."

Shortly, Colonel Malenkov, a trim, dignified figure who always looked composed in an immaculate uniform, appeared. "This lieutenant urgently needs a complete examination."

"Dmitri Vasilyevich, only two weeks ago I myself gave Lieutenant Belenko a complete physical examination."

"This will be a psychiatric examination. It is clear to me that this officer is insane. I am sure that is what the examination will find."

Belenko, clad in a ragged robe, was locked alone in a hospital room. Nobody, not even the orderlies who brought the repugnant rations which must have come from the soldiers' mess, spoke to him. Probably the solitary confinement was meant to intimidate him, but it afforded him sufficient respite to realize that he must say or do nothing which might give anybody grounds for labeling him insane.

On the third morning he was led to Malenkov's office, and the doctor shut the door behind him. The pilots liked Malenkov because they felt he appreciated both their mentality and frustrations. He had been a combat infantryman in World War II, then trained as a physician, not because he wanted to be a physician—he yearned to be an architect—but because the Party needed doctors. He had served the Party as a military doctor for a quarter of a century. Asked what had happened, Belenko explained, and they talked nearly an hour.

"Viktor Ivanovich, I know you are all right. I know that what you say is true; at least, I have knowledge of some of the incidents you describe. But why try to piss into the wind? If you want to live in shit the rest of your life, go ahead and express your feelings. If you want to sleep on clean sheets and eat white bread with butter, you must learn to repress your feelings and pay lip service.

"Golodnikov is not a bad fellow; he's a friend of mine. You drove him into a corner, and you have to let him out. If I tell him you were temporarily fatigued from overwork, that you recognize your mistake, that you regret it, that you will pursue this no further, I'm reasonably sure it all will be forgotten. Why don't we do that?"

If I do that, I always will know that I am a coward. For what purpose do I live? To grovel and lie so I may eat white bread? What would Spartacus do?

"I will not do that. I will tell the truth."

Malenkov sighed. "Oh, Viktor Ivanovich. Now you drive *me* into a corner. What can I do? I will have to tell the truth, too, and try to help you. But we still will have to go through with the psychiatric examination."

Although Malenkov could have chosen a local psychiatrist or a military psychiatrist, he instead drove Belenko to the medical institute in Stavropol, one hundred miles away. There he had a personal friend, an eminent psychiatrist whose name Belenko never caught. As they entered, he said, "All you have to do is relax and tell the truth."

The psychiatrist and Malenkov talked alone some twenty minutes before calling in Belenko. "Well, well, what do we have here?" he asked Belenko, who as factually as he knew how reported his confrontation with Golodnikov. "Why, we have an open rebellion! Nothing less," exclaimed the psychiatrist. "You must be very distraught or very brave."

For an hour and then, after a brief pause, another two hours the psychiatrist questioned Belenko about all aspects of his life, from early childhood to the present. Neither his mannerisms nor wording disclosed anything to Belenko about his reactions to the answers, and until the last few seconds Belenko did not know whether he had "passed" the examination.

"So, Lieutenant, tell me. Just what is it that you want?"

"I want to be a fighter pilot. I want to grow professionally.

Most of all, I want to get away from all this lying, corruption, and hypocrisy."

"Well, that seems to me like a healthy, progressive ambition. We shall see. You may go now."

Escorting Belenko to the door, the psychiatrist extended his hand and gripped Belenko's very hard. In a half whisper he said, "Good luck, Lieutenant. Don't worry."

Four days later Belenko learned the results of the examination entirely by chance from an Armavir classmate who was visiting the base with an inspection team. An ear problem had forced him to quit flying, and he worked in the personnel center of the Air Defense Command. When he offered congratulations, Belenko asked what he meant.

"Haven't you been told? You're going to a MiG-25 squadron in the Far East. The general here gave you a fantastic recommendation. Said you're such an outstanding pilot you belong in our most modern aircraft. You must have been licking his ass every day the past four years."

Belenko did not ask whether the records mentioned the psychiatric examination. Obviously they did not. Doubtless Malenkov and/or the psychiatrist had convinced Golodnikov that in the interests of his self-preservation he had better give Belenko what he asked and ship him as far away as possible as soon as possible.

Belenko was thankful for the transfer but unmollified and unforgiving, and in the days preceding his departure, his bitterness swelled. While he was away, word had spread or had been spread that he was insane. Krotkov, the guitar player, and a couple of other instructors welcomed him. Everybody else avoided him; they feared to be seen near him. He thought of scenes in *The Call of the Wild.* If a husky in a dogsled team was helplessly wounded, accidentally or in a fight, the other huskies, along whose side it had toiled, would turn on it as one and devour it.

I knew them as individual human beings. Now they act like a pack of animals. Our system makes them that way.

There is nothing I can say to them. There is no way I can

defend myself, against them or our system. There is no way any-
body can defend himself. If it hadn't been for Malenkov, I'd be in
a lunatic asylum right now. If our system can do that to me, it
can do it to anybody.

He was not conscious of it at the time. But within him the
dam that contained the poisonous doubts, the disastrous conclusions, the recurrent rage had burst, and nothing could repair it. In a sense different from that in which they were spoken, the words of Golodnikov did apply. For Belenko it indeed
was now too late.

Ludmilla cried every day their first week or so in
Chuguyevka, 120 miles northeast of Vladivostok, almost a
continent away from Salsk. By comparison with this village of
2,000 souls, isolated in forests not far from Korea to the south
and Manchuria to the west, Salsk, which she so despised,
seemed glittering and glamorous. The streets were unlighted
and unpaved, the frame houses were unpainted, the outhouses and open garbage pits in their yards buzzed with flies
and crawled with worms, and the whole place stank as bad as
the poorest *kolkhoz* on the hottest summer day. The social
center of the village was Café No. 2, popular because it sold
beer which local entrepreneurs imported from Vladivostok.
The patrons laced the beer with vodka, and because of the
effects of overindulgence, the café also reeked. Sausage and
meat were unavailable in the three stores, and fruit and vegetables also were scarce except at the bazaar on Sunday.

A sawmill was the main employer of the village. A few
citizens, among them a number of Ukrainians exiled to the
Far East for life, worked as supervisors at a *kolkhoz* a couple of
miles away or at the chemical factory on the outskirts. Elec-
trified barbed-wire fences guarded the chemical factory, the
labor force of which was composed of *zeks*. They were
marched in each morning in a column, their shaved heads
bowed, their hands clasped behind their backs, watched
by dogs and guards with machine guns. Their rags, their
canvas boots, their forlorn, empty eyes were the same as

those Belenko remembered seeing twenty years before in Rubtsovsk.

A few days after Belenko reported to the base seven miles from the village, the commandant, Lieutenant Colonel Yevgeny Ivanovich Shevsov, and the chief political officer convened all pilots and officers in a secret meeting. To Belenko, their candor bespoke desperation.

"Drunkenness induced by aircraft alcohol is constant and widespread," they said. "The soldiers are running away from the base and taking girls from the villages away into the forests for days. Several times the soldiers have refused to eat their food. We have had strikes here! We have brawls among the soldiers, and to our shame, some officers have been involved in them. Soldiers are writing letters to their parents about what a horrible situation we have here, and the Organs of State Security have been investigating. At any time we could have an inspection. If there is an inspection, it will show that this regiment is not combat-ready. Our planes often cannot fly because everybody is so drunk or people have run away.

"Each of you is responsible. You must concentrate your attention on the soldiers. Explain to them that our difficulties are temporary and will be eliminated eventually. Tell them that our country is not yet rich enough to build planes and barracks at the same time. Emphasize that the Dark Forces of the West have enlisted the Chinese and Japanese in their plot to kidnap our Mother Country."

How many times, thousands of times, have I heard that the Dark Forces want to kidnap our Mother Country? Do they want our food? That is very funny. They are starving, but they sell us wheat to keep us from starving. Our system is the best, but we want to learn to grow corn and fly and do everything else just as they do. Do we have anything that they want? That anybody wants?

The collapse of morale and discipline and the resultant chaos were outgrowths of a massive and urgent military buildup progressing throughout the Soviet Far East. At Chuguyevka three squadrons of MiG-25s (thirty-six combat aircraft plus four or five modified with twin seats as trainers) were replacing three MiG-17 squadrons. A far more complex aircraft, one MiG-25 required four to five times more support personnel—engineers, mechanics, electronics, and armament specialists—than a MiG-17. Within the previous two months the number of officers and men at Chuguyevka had quadrupled, and more were arriving weekly. But no provision whatsoever had been made to expand housing, dining, or any other facilities to accommodate the enormous influx of people.

Belenko and Ludmilla were comparatively lucky in that they shared a two-room apartment with only one family, a flight engineer, his wife, and two children. Other apartments were packed with three or four families of officers, and despite the best of will, conflicts over use of the bathroom and kitchen inevitably arose, afflicting everyone with strain and tension. Ludmilla was able to work part time as a nurse at the base dispensary, but for most other wives, some of whom were teachers or engineers, employment opportunities were nil.

Each pilot periodically stood watch as duty officer for twenty-four hours, during which he supervised the enlisted personnel, inspected the barracks and mess hall, and generally tried to enforce discipline. What Belenko saw on his first watch appalled him.

Between 180 and 200 men were jammed into barracks marginally adequate for 40. Bunks stood in tiers nearly against each other, and the congestion was such that it was difficult to move without stumbling into somebody. There were two water faucets in each barracks, the toilet was outside, and sometimes during the night men relieved themselves in their neighbor's boots. They were given a change of underwear once a week and allowed to go into the village for a steam bath once every ten days, there being no bathhouse on the base.

Comparable congestion in the mess hall made cleanliness impossible, and the place smelled like a garbage pit. While one section of forty men ate, another forty stood behind them waiting to take places and plates. If they chose, they then could wait in line to dip the plate in a pan of cold water containing no soap. Usually they elected simply to brush the plate off with their hands. For breakfast the men received 150 grams of bread, 10 grams of butter, 20 grams of sugar, barley mush cooked with water, and a mug of tea. Dinner consisted of thin soup, sometimes thickened with cereal, buckwheat groats, perhaps a piece or two of fatback, and a mug of kissel, a kind of starchy gelatin. Supper was the same as breakfast.

Except for a television set, no recreational facilities of any kind were available to the enlisted men (or the officers, for that matter), and there was little they could do. There was much they were forbidden to do. They were forbidden to listen to a transistor radio, to draw pictures of women, to listen to records, to read fiction, to write letters about their life in the service, to lie or sit on their bunks during their free time (there was no place else to sit), to watch television except when political or patriotic programs were shown, and to drink. But drink they did, in staggering quantities, for alcohol was the one commodity available in limitless amounts.

To fly seventy minutes, the maximum time it can stay aloft without refueling, a MiG-25 needs fourteen tons of jet fuel and one-half ton of alcohol for braking and electronic systems. So wherever MiG-25s were based, huge quantities of alcohol were stored, and in the Soviet Air Force the plane was popularly known as the Flying Restaurant. And officers from surrounding bases—Air Force, Army, political officers—seized on any pretext to visit Chuguyevka and fill their bottles.

According to a story circulated at Chuguyevka, a group of Air Force wives, distraught over their husbands' habitual drunkenness, staged a protest at a design bureau in Moscow, appealing to it to design aircraft that would not use alcohol. Supposedly a representative of the bureau told the ladies, "Go screw yourselves. If we want, we will fuel our planes with cognac."

In April 1976 Belenko's squadron commander asked him to take a truck and pick up a shipment of office supplies from a railroad freight terminal thirty miles north of Vladivostok, paper and office supplies being essential to the functioning of the squadron. It was a task that should have been performed by the deputy squadron commander, but he never stayed sober enough to be trusted with the truck.

The morning was bright, the dirt road empty and not yet dusty, and forests through which he drove were awesome in their natural, unspoiled beauty. They reminded him of man's capacity to despoil nature and himself and of delicious hours in other forests.

Starting back, Belenko saw a frail, ragged figure walking along the road, and the man looked so forlorn he decided to give him a lift. The hitchhiker, who had few teeth, gaunt eyes, sparse hair, and a sallow, unhealthy complexion, looked to be in his sixties. He explained that he worked at the freight terminal and walked or hitchhiked daily to and from his hut eight miles down the road.

"How long have you been here?"

"Almost twenty-five years. After the war I spent ten years in the camps, and ever since, I've worked around here, doing whatever I could find. I am not allowed to go back to the Ukraine, although I miss my home very much. I have relatives, but it is too expensive for them to visit me. You know how life is. The first years were very hard for me because it is so cold here. The Ukraine is warm and sunny, you know, and there are flowers and fruit. I wish I could see it once more before I die. But I guess I won't. I have no passport."*

"How old are you?"

"Forty-seven."

---

* To legally travel from one locale to another, each Soviet citizen must possess an internal passport which is issued or denied at the discretion of the authorities. Denial or withdrawal of a passport effectively confines a person to the area of his residence indefinitely.

"Are you married?"

"Oh, yes. She spent eight years in the camps. She's also from the Ukraine. Her relatives were exiled. They've all died now, and there's just the two of us. We thought about children, but we were afraid we couldn't take care of them. It's not easy to get a good job if you're an exile. You know how life is."

"What did you do? Did you kill someone?"

"No, I gave bread to the men from the forest."*

What can he do, that poor man, to our country? Look at him. He hardly has any teeth; he won't live much longer. What kind of enemy is he? What kind of criminal? Whatever he did, ten years are punishment enough. Why not let him go back to his home and die? Why be so hateful? What kind of freedom do we have here?

Belenko was sent to a training center near Moscow for a few weeks' intensive study of the MiG-25, and when he returned in mid-June, a state of emergency existed in Chuguyevka. A dysentery epidemic had disabled fully 40 percent of the regiment, two soldiers had committed suicide, at least twenty had deserted, there had been more hunger strikes, and the enlisted men now were verging on open mutiny. Fuel shortages had prevented pilots from flying as much as they needed to master their new aircraft. American reconnaissance planes, SR-71s, were prowling off the coast, staying just outside Soviet airspace but photographing terrain hundreds of miles inland with side-angle cameras. They taunted and toyed with the MiG-25s sent up to intercept them, scooting up to altitudes the Soviet planes could not reach, and circling leisurely above them or dashing off at speeds the Russians could not match. Moscow was incensed, and Commandant Shevsov lived in terror of an investigation.

---

* The "men from the forest" were Ukrainian nationalists, followers of General Stefan Bandera, who allied themselves with the Germans in World War II and afterward tenaciously continued guerrilla warfare against the communists until they were largely wiped out in the late 1940s. Bandera escaped to West Germany but was killed there in 1959 by a KGB assassin.

Already they had been notified that the regional political officer was flying in next week to lecture all officers of the regiment.

Shevsov announced that a pilot from each squadron would have to speak at the scheduled assembly, present an assessment of the regiment's problems, and propose solutions. He instructed his political officer to pick those likely to create the most favorable impression. The regimental political officer was not from the political directorate of the armed forces; rather, he was a pilot who in the frenzied formation of the regiment just happened to be saddled with the job. He thought as a pilot, and he was the only popular political officer Belenko ever knew. When asked, Belenko told him bluntly and in detail what he thought was wrong and what should be done.

"Well, I agree. You will speak for your squadron. If you say just what you said to me, maybe it will shock them into letting us do something."

The regional political officer, a corpulent, perfumed man with bags under his eyes, appeared in a resplendent uniform bedecked with medals that made the pilots smile at each other because they knew that no political officer had ever participated in battle, except perhaps at a bar.

"Comrade Officers, your regiment is in a serious situation, a desperate situation.

"Around us the SR-71 is flying, spying on us, watching us in the day and in the night.

"The Chinese are a day's walk away from us. We should not let the Chinese frighten us. We can massacre them any-time we want. They have a few nuclear bombs, but they can deliver them only by donkey. Their planes are so old we can wipe them out of the sky. But we cannot underestimate the Chinese because there are so many of them, and they are fanatical, mad. If we kill a million of them a day, we still will have three years of work ahead of us.

"So the Party requires that you increase your vigilance, your readiness, your discipline in order to defend our Mother

Country. You have been given our country's best interceptor. It has the highest speed and the highest altitude of any plane we have. It is a very good weapon. Yet your regiment is in such disgraceful condition that you cannot use this weapon properly. Your soldiers and, yes, some officers, too, are drinking the alcohol for the planes, and your regiment is too drunk to defend our Mother Country."

We know all that. We've heard all that. It's as if they sent us a recording instead of a man.

Belenko was the fifth member of the regiment to speak, following Shevsov, the deputy regimental commander, and two other pilots.

"We must consider our problems in light of the principles of Marxism/Leninism and the science of communism," he began. "These principles teach us that man is a product of his environment. If we examine the environment in which we have placed our men, we can see the origins of our problems and perhaps, in the origins, some solutions.

"On the *kolkhoz* I have seen livestock housed better than our men are housed. I have seen pigs fed better than our men are fed. There is no place for our men to wash themselves. That and the filthy mess hall are why we have so much dysentery. There is no place for our men to play, and they are forbidden to do almost anything that a normal young man would want to do. We have created for them an environment from which any normal person would want to escape, so they try to escape through alcohol.

"We must change that environment. First of all, we must build decent barracks, a decent mess hall, a decent latrine, and a bathhouse with fire for hot water. There are nearly eight hundred of us here. If we all went to work, officers, sergeants, soldiers, we could do that in a month. If there is not enough money, let us go into the forest and cut the logs ourselves. If every officer would contribute 30 rubles from his salary, we would have more than six thousand rubles to buy other materials.

"We should organize social parties at the base and invite

students so that our men can meet nice girls in a normal way. It is unnatural and unhealthy to try to keep our men from seeing girls.

"The forests and streams are full of deer, elk, rabbits, ducks, geese, quail, and fish. We should take our men to hunt and fish. It would be enjoyable for them, and the game would enrich their diet. We should start our own garden and plant our own potatoes right here on the base.

"Each weekend officers should be appointed to take groups of men on the train into Vladivostok and let them just walk around the city. We can ride the train free, and we can sleep in the station, and we can take up a collection among the officers to buy them some sausage and beer instead of vodka. It will give them something to look forward to. It will show that we care about them.

"When we can, we should build a football field and a library so the men can improve their professional skills and education. And if they want to read detective stories, why not let them? That's better than having them drink alcohol.

"If we demonstrate to our men that we are loyal to them, that we respect them, then they will be loyal and respect us and obey us. If we give them alternatives to alcohol, most will take those alternatives.

"Comrade Colonel, I have spoken frankly in the hope that my views will be of use to our regiment and our Mother Country."

As Belenko sat down, the officers clapped their hands, whistled, stomped their feet, pounded the table until Shevsov stood and silenced them.

The visiting political officer, who had been taking notes, rose, his face fixed with a waxen smile.

"Comrade Officers, this has been a productive gathering. I find some merit in what each of you has said. I find that underneath, this regiment is imbued with determination to eliminate drunkenness, to enforce discipline, and to serve our Mother Country. That is what I shall report.

"But to you, Comrade Belenko, I must say a few words

frankly, just as you spoke frankly. You do not ask, 'What may I give to the Party?' You ask the Party to give, give, give; give me utopia, now. You show that you lack the imagination to grasp the magnitude of the problem, much less the difficulty of solving it. You do not understand that our country cannot build complex aircraft, modern airfields, and barracks all at the same time, and your priorities are exactly the reverse of what they should be. You spoke of the principles of Marxism/Leninism. I urge you to restudy these principles until you understand that the Party and the people are one and that, therefore, the needs of the Party always must be first. We will do everything in time, step by step, and the Party wisely has decided which steps must be taken first, threatened as we are by the Chinese and the Dark Forces of the West."

The faintest of hopes, the tiniest flicker of light sparked by Belenko's speech evaporated. Nothing would be done. They filed out silently, Shevsov among them and for once one of them.

Pig! No, that is an insult to a pig. In the order of the universe, a pig serves some useful purpose. You and all you stand for are to the universe like cancer.

I wish I could put you for one night in those barracks and see how you feel when someone shits in your boot. I wish I could march you into that mess hall where a maggot would retch. Oh, there you would learn the science of communism.

Well, go back to your fresh fruits and meat and perfume and lying while our men lie disabled by dysentery, cholera, and alcohol, while the Americans look down and laugh at us from the skies. But you leave me alone.

All my life I have tried to understand, tried to believe you. I understand now. Our system is rotten, hopelessly, incurably rotten. Everything that is wrong is not the result of mistakes by bureaucrats in this town or that; it is the results of our system. I don't understand what is wrong; but it is wrong. It produced you. You, not the Dark Forces, have kidnapped our Mother Country.

Soon after this climactic and decisive intellectual rebellion, Ludmilla announced that she was leaving. They had tried as best two people could; they had failed; it was pointless to try anew. Her parents were overjoyed by the prospect of having her and Dmitri with them in Magadan, and they could guarantee Dmitri's future and hers. She would stay until October, when her commitment to the dispensary expired. But after she left it would be best for all if he never saw her or Dmitri, who would only be confused by his reappearance.

Her statement was so dispassionate and consistent with previous demands for divorce that Belenko could find neither energy nor desire to try anew to dissuade her. Besides, she was right about Dmitri.

Conditions at Chuguyevka were not atypical of those throughout the Far East. Reports of desertions, suicides, disease, and rampant alcoholism were said to be flooding into Moscow from bases all over. In late June, Shevsov convened the officers in an Absolutely Secret meeting to convey grave news. At an Army base only thirty-five miles to the southwest, two soldiers had killed two other soldiers and an officer, confiscated machine guns and provisions, and struck out through the forest toward the coast, intending to steal a boat and sail to Japan. They dodged and fought pursuing patrols several days until they were killed, and on their bodies were found diaries containing vile slanders of the Soviet Army and the grossest misrepresentations of the life of a soldier. These diaries atop all the reports of trouble had caused such concern in Moscow that the Minister of Defense himself was coming to the Far East and to Chuguyevka.

The career of every officer would depend on his impressions, and to make a good impression, it would be necessary to build a paved road from the base to the helicopter pad where the Minister would land, about four miles away. The entire regiment would begin work on the road tomorrow.

It never was clear just where in the chain of command the order originated; certainly Shevsov had no authority to initiate such a costly undertaking. In any case, the Dark Forces, the SR-71s, the Chinese, the desirability of maintaining flying proficiency—all were forgotten now. Pilots, engineers, technicians, mechanics, cooks, everybody turned to road building—digging a base, laying gravel, pouring concrete, and covering it with macadam.

It's unbelievable. For this we could have built everything, barracks, mess hall, everything. We could have built a palace!

But the crowning order was yet to come. Within a radius of about a mile, the land around the base had been cleared of trees to facilitate takeoffs and landings. The Minister, it was said, was a devotee of nature and its verdancy. He would want to see green trees as he rode to the base. Therefore, trees would have to be transplanted to line the mile or so of road.

You can't transplant trees here in the middle of the summer! Everybody knows that!

But transplanted they were, hundreds of them, pines, spruces, poplars, dug up from the forest, hauled by truck and placed every fifteen yards along the road. By the first week in July they were dead, shriveling and yellowing.

Dig them up and replace them. So they did, with the same results.

Do it again. He may be here anytime now.

So again saplings and some fairly tall trees were imported by the hundreds from the forests. Again they all died. Finally acknowledging that nature would not change its ways for them, someone had an idea. Leave them there, and just before he arrives, we'll spray them all with green paint. We'll drive fast, and he won't know the difference.

It all was to no avail. In early August they were advised that illness had forced cancellation of the Minister's inspection. He wasn't coming after all. It was time to fly again.

To fly well and safely, a pilot must practice regularly. His skills, like muscles, grow flabby and can even atrophy through disuse. Because of fuel shortages and preoccupation with the road, they had flown little since May.

The second day they resumed, a pilot suffered vertigo as he descended through clouds preparatory to landing. In his disorientation he panicked and ejected himself. Scrub one MiG-25 and the millions of rubles it cost.

Subsequently a MiG-25 malfunctioned at takeoff. The runway was conspicuously marked by a line and guideposts. If a plane was not airborne upon reaching this line, the pilot was supposed to abort the takeoff, deploy his drag chute immediately, brake the aircraft; if he did, he could stop in time. But on this morning the pilot neglected to abort soon enough, and the MiG-25 plunged headlong off the runway. By terrible misfortune a civilian bus was passing, and like a great steel knife, the wing of the MiG sheared off the top third of the bus, decapitating or dismembering five children, three women, and two men and badly injuring other passengers. When Belenko went to help, he saw three soldiers from the rescue party lying on the ground, having fainted at the horror of the sight.

The crashes might have occurred in any circumstances, even if the pilots had been flying regularly, even if they were not fatigued from working twelve hours a day seven days a week on the road. But Belenko did not think so. *It was murder.*

That night he knew it was futile to try to sleep, futile to try to postpone a decision any longer. A fever of the spirit possessed him, and only by a decision could he attain relief. He told Ludmilla that he had to return to the base, and through the night he wandered beneath the moonlight in the forests.

For hours, thoughts, recollections, apprehensions—half-formed, disjointed, uncongealed, contradictory, disorderly—tumbled chaotically through his mind until he realized that, as in other crises, he must gather sufficient strength, courage, and poise to think logically.

I cannot live under this system. For me there can be no purpose or meaning to life under this system. I cannot change this system. I cannot overthrow it. I might escape it. If I escaped it, I might hurt it.

Why should I not try? I will have no family. Mother I have not heard from in twenty-five years. Father I have not seen for eight years. They are not like father and mother to me anyway. Ludmilla does not want to see me again. Dmitri, maybe I could see him a few times in my life, but we would be strangers. Privilege, yes, I have privilege; I could retire in 1987. But was I born to think only about whether I eat meat and white bread? No, I was born to find my way, to understand; to understand, you must be free.

Is there freedom in the West, in America? What would it be like there? I don't know. I know they have lied about everything else, so maybe they have lied about the West, about the Dark Forces. I know that however bad it is in the West, it cannot be worse than here. If the Dark Forces are the way they say, I can always kill myself; if they are as bad as they say, there is no hope for the world or mankind.

All right. I will try. And I will try to hurt this system as badly as I can. I will try to give the Dark Forces what this system most wants to keep secret from them. I will give them my plane and all its secrets.

The fever had broken, replaced by a serenity, a purposefulness exceeding any he ever had known.

On a navigation map Belenko drew from Chuguyevka an arc representing the maximum range he estimated he could expect to attain, considering the evasive maneuvers and altitudes he would have to fly. Within the arc he discerned only one potentially hospitable airfield large enough to accommodate a MiG-25, the military field at Chitose on the Japanese island of Hokkaido. *All right. It has to be Chitose.*

He could not attempt the flight until two conditions obtained simultaneously: The planes had to be fully fueled, and the weather very good. Because a MiG-25 cannot land safely with much fuel aboard, they were not loaded to capacity unless they were going to try to intercept the SR-71s or engage in an important exercise such as the firing of missiles. To prevent MiG-25 pilots from talking with foreign pilots, the radios were restricted to a very narrow frequency band that permitted communications only with other MiGs and Ground Control. Thus, he would be unable to tell the Japanese of his intentions or to ask their guidance. He could only hope that Japanese interceptors would force him down or that he could locate the field himself. In either case, clear weather was essential.

Any commander had the right at any time to ask a pilot the most recondite technical questions about his aircraft, tactics, production, or any other professional matter. To prepare himself for these quizzes, Belenko kept notes in a thick tablet which he carried in a flap pocket of his flight suit. Now he began methodically and cryptically recording in the tablet every Soviet military secret he had ever heard, every thought, and all data that might be beneficial to the United States.

There was one more thing to do. It was imperative that as soon as he landed, the Japanese take all measures necessary to protect the MiG-25 and prevent its recovery by the Russians. He wanted to tell them that, but he could speak not a word of Japanese or English. So he decided that he must write a message in English to hand to the first Japanese official he met. He drafted the message first in Russian: "Immediately contact a representative of the American intelligence service. Conceal and guard the aircraft at once. Do not allow anyone near it." Laboriously, with the aid of a little Russian-English dictionary, he translated as best he could the message into English.

That done, he could do nothing more except wait for the day, not knowing when it might come. He knew that when it came, the chances would be very much against him. But he was at peace with himself. For the moment he had found a purpose.

In a Japanese Prison

Barely maintaining airspeed, Belenko slid the MiG-25 downward through the seemingly interminable darkness of the clouds, each second of descent diminishing the chances of success and survival. He watched the altimeter . . . , 600 meters . . . , 500 . . . , 400 . . . , 300 . . . , ...

I'll pull up at one-fifty if I'm still in the clouds. Any lower would be suicide.

At 250 meters, the world lit up; he was under the clouds and could see . . . an airfield. It was not the base of Chitose he sought but the commercial airport at Hakodate, ninety miles to the southwest. The runway was shorter by a third than any on which he had ever landed a MiG-25, and he knew it would be impossible to stop on the field. But maybe he could keep the plane and himself largely intact.

He banked steeply to the right, turned about 260 degrees, and began his approach toward the south end of the runway. Then, within seconds, he had to make an excruciating choice. A Japanese airliner, a Boeing 727, was taking off, right into his flight path. The gauge showed empty, and he could not be sure that he had enough fuel to circle again for another approach. If the fuel ran out and he lost power during another turn, the aircraft would plummet straight down like a twenty-two-ton boulder and smash itself into mostly worthless pieces. If he continued his approach, he might collide with the airliner, and the range between it and the MiG-25 was closing so rapidly that neither the commercial pilot nor he would have any margin for a mistake.

No, I cannot do that. I was not born to kill those people. Whatever I think, I do not have that right. Better one life than many.

He jerked the MiG into the tightest turn of which it was capable, allowed the 727 to clear, dived at a dangerously sharp angle, and touched the runway at 220 knots. As he deployed the drag chute and repeatedly slammed down the brake pedal, the MiG bucked, bridled, and vibrated, as if it were going to come apart. Tires burning, it screeched and skidded down the runway, slowing but not stopping. It ran off the north end of the field, knocked down a pole, plowed over a second and finally stopped a few feet from a large antenna 800 feet off the runway. The front tire had blown, but that was all. The tanks contained enough fuel for about thirty more seconds of powered flight.

Belenko was conscious of no emotions: no sense of triumph, no relief at being alive. There was no time for emotion, just as there had been no time in the air.

Get out! Protect the aircraft! Find the Americans! Act! Now!

He ripped off his oxygen mask, unharnessed the parachute, slid back the canopy, and climbed out on the wing. The plane had come to rest near a highway, cars were pulling over, and motorists hopping out with their cameras. Schooled for years in secrecy, drilled to understand that a MiG-25 represented one of the most important state secrets, Belenko impulsively reacted as if he still were in the Soviet Union.

You may not do that! This aircraft is absolutely secret! The taking of pictures is strictly forbidden! Stop!

Unable to communicate by words, he whipped out his pistol and fired into the air. In Japan the possession or discharge of firearms is a grave, almost unheard-of crime, and had he detonated a small bomb, the effects on the onlookers would not have been more traumatic. They immediately lowered their cameras; some took out the film and tossed it on the ground before him.

A procession of three cars drove slowly down the runway and halted prudently out of pistol range. Two men got out and approached warily, holding high a white flag. They kept pointing and gesturing toward the pistol until he put it back in the holster. Only then did one of the Japanese come close enough to talk. Belenko jumped off the wing to meet him.

"Do you speak English?"

"*Nyet.*"

The Japanese waved to his companion, a very elderly little man, who walked forward and addressed Belenko in pidgin Russian. "Pistoly, pleezy." Belenko handed him the pistol. "And knify, too." He surrendered the knife protruding from a flap pocket of his flight suit. "Follow us, pleezy. Do not wolly."

Near pandemonium reigned in the airport terminal as crowds of people strained and shoved to see, to try to touch this exotic being who so suddenly and unexpectedly had landed in their midst from another world. When Belenko entered, a Japanese stood by the door, holding a handsome aircraft manual open to a page displaying a drawing of a MiG-25. Grinning and nodding his head rapidly, he held out the manual before Belenko, as if to ask, "Am I right?"

Yes, nodded Belenko. The man put down the manual, grinned more broadly, and clapped.

Within ten minutes after Belenko landed, the Japanese had summoned an official who spoke Russian superbly. Although he introduced himself as a representative of the Japanese Foreign Office, Belenko suspected that he was an intelligence officer. In the office of the airport manager Belenko gave him the note he so laboriously had attempted to write in English precisely for an occasion such as this.

"Who wrote this?" the Japanese official asked.

"I did."

"Good! Now, tell me how it happened. Did you lose your way?"

"No, I did not. I flew here on purpose. I am asking political asylum in the United States. Conceal the aircraft, and place guards around it at once. Call the Americans immediately."

As soon as the official translated, the other Japanese started cheering, and some danced about the office. "All right! All right!" the official shouted.

"Would you mind writing down in your own words again just what you have told me?"

"I will do that gladly."

"Follow us," they said, and Belenko did so, pulling his jacket over his head to avoid being photographed by the newsmen who had flocked to the scene. Through a narrow corridor they hurried outside to a waiting car, which sped them along back streets to the rear entrance of a hotel.

An interpreter and two security men stayed with Belenko inside the hotel room while two sentries stood guard outside the door. They presented him with new underwear, a kimono, and shoes, packed away all the clothes he wore, and suggested he take a shower.

They must think I smell bad. That's right, everything smells so clean here.

A dinner of eight different dishes—meat, fish, poultry, vegetables, and rice—was served in the room. All the tastes were new to Belenko, and all delicious. "I heard you have very good beer in Japan," he said hopefully.

"Thank you, but in the present circumstances, we cannot allow you any alcohol." Although the Japanese did not tell him, the Russians were already accusing them of drugging a lost Soviet pilot, and they were fearful of lending the remotest substance to the allegations.

Another representative of the Japanese Foreign Office, a poised, confident, and well-dressed man in his thirties, visited the room about 9:00 P.M. In fluent Russian he asked Belenko to repeat the details and purpose of his flight. Having done so, Belenko instructed, "Take my parachute and clothes, and drop them in the sea to make them think there was a crash."

"I am sorry; that is quite impossible. The news is everywhere, all over the world. Now the Russians are demanding that we return you and your plane. But we will not return you. You do not have to worry. You will be very safe, and we will do all you have asked. It will take a while because of red tape. Have you heard this phrase 'red tape'? There are bureaucrats everywhere."

"Yes, I know about bureaucrats."

"Tomorrow you will go to Tokyo. For your security we will use a military plane."

"I am ready."

The Japanese shook hands and rose to leave. "You cannot realize how great an incident you have created for Japan, the Soviet Union, and the United States. We are under the greatest pressure from the Russians. But we will not deliver you to them because that would be contrary to our law and our democracy. Do not worry."

He is sincere. That is what they mean now. But what if they cannot stand the Soviet pressure? No, I believe him. I must believe him.

He slept poorly and noticed that the security men sitting on the other bed were replaced about 2:00 A.M. Early in the morning they brought him a suit; the jacket fitted, but the pants were too small. They sent out for another; the pants fitted, but were too long, and the jacket was far too large. There being no more time for fittings, the Japanese fetched some scissors and shortened the pants by six inches. Attired in pants that now extended barely to his socks, a drooping coat, a funny hat that was too big, and dark glasses, he looked very much like a clown.

They exited through the hotel kitchen into an alley, but swarms of reporters and photographers had anticipated them. The security men bulled through the journalists, hustled him into a car, and raced away with the press in pursuit.

Approaching a large intersection, the official Japanese cars maneuvered until they were five abreast, then at the intersection dashed away in different directions, confusing the press as to which should be followed. By a circuitous route, Belenko arrived at a garbage dump outside town, and a helicopter swooped down. In thirty seconds he was flying away.

The helicopter set down at the Chitose base next to a military transport whose engines were running, and as soon as Belenko and his escorts boarded, it took off. Because of noise in the plane, designed to carry freight rather than people, conversation was difficult, and during most of the flight Belenko gazed in solitude and marveled at the Japanese landscape. Every inch of arable land, even precipitous slopes, appeared to be meticulously cultivated. Towns and villages looked neat and orderly. Nowhere was waste or spoliation visible. The whole countryside looked to him like a beautiful and lovingly tended garden.

How paradoxical the world is. The Japanese have little land, few resources. But look what they have done with them. I can see for myself.

At the airport outside Tokyo another horde of aggressive photographers and reporters blocked their way, and camera flashes momentarily blinded Belenko. Again, security men shoved through the mob, and they sped away in a convoy of cars, pursued by the journalists on motorcycles. The chase astounded Belenko. The security officers and police were communicating with radios smaller than their hands, activated, he guessed by the same kinds of transistors the Russians had to steal from the Japanese to equip MiGs. The reporters also had the little radios and were tracking the motorcade by monitoring the police frequencies.

How can this be? Why, if this happened in the Soviet Union, the KGB would catch those journalists and send them to the camps for espionage.

The official cars swerved to the curb, and a Japanese jumped out and ran to a telephone booth to make a secure call by landline. After he returned and they drove off, the interpreter explained. "We are so sorry, but it has been decided that we must take you to a prison. We have no other place where we can guarantee your security. At the moment the prison will be the safest place for you in Tokyo."

By means similar to those employed in Hakodate, they eluded the pursuit at a traffic circle, the cars peeling off down different streets, and about ten minutes later they entered a naval compound. "There is an American here who wishes to speak with you."

The Dark Forces. I'm going to meet the Dark Forces. What will they be like? What will they do with me?

The American, dressed in a three-piece gray suit, a white shirt with a button-down collar, a striped tie, and black shoes, stood up and offered his hand when Belenko entered the office of the base commandant. He was slender, had sandy hair and a fair complexion, and wore glasses. "My name is Jim, and I represent the United States government," he said in flawless Russian. "It is a pleasure to meet you and an honor to inform you that the President of the United States has granted your request for political asylum. You have nothing to worry about. As soon as the necessary bureaucratic procedures are completed, you will fly to the States. It won't be long.

"Do you have any questions or requests? Is there anything you would like to say?"

"No. I understand everything."

"All right. Take good care of yourself. I will see you soon, and we will be able to talk more freely later."

Somehow Belenko had expected more, something dramatic, even epic, and he was vaguely disappointed that his first encounter with an American had been so simple, almost casual.

The Dark Forces, they seem very peaceful. Maybe they are just being clever in a way I don't know.

Repeatedly apologizing for the character of his lodging, the Japanese exerted themselves to make Belenko feel comfortable and welcome. They laid mattresses on the floor of his cell, brought pillows, sheets, and blankets, wheeled in a color television set, gave him a chess board, invited him to work out in the gym or use the steam bath. They emphasized over and over that the guards, who would stand by him every minute of the day and night and even accompany him to the bathroom, were his protectors, not his captors. And that evening they served him a multicourse dinner that was the best he ever had eaten.

Thinking that a banquet had been especially prepared for him, he asked who the chef was. The Japanese said they simply had ordered the food from a common café across the street from the compound.

"Really!" Belenko blurted. "I heard you were all starving over here."

After dinner he luxuriated in the steam bath and, for the first time since strapping himself into the cockpit at Chuguyevka, he relaxed. His two guards were beaming when he emerged, clad in a silk kimono and sandals. Exhausted as he was, he craved exercise and started toward the gym, but they tugged at his sleeve and pointed him back toward the cell. Someone had procured for him a half-liter bottle of cold Japanese beer. It was even better than its reputation. He slept profoundly even though the guards kept the cell and corridor fully illuminated throughout the night.

The second morning in Tokyo the Japanese dumbfounded him with an announcement that he would have to stand trial for breaking their laws. He could not quite believe what was happening as they led him into an office of the prison, where a robed judge greeted him with a formal statement, translated by an aged interpreter.

"You are accused of breaking the laws of Japan on four counts. You illegally intruded on our airspace. You entered our country without a visa. You carried a pistol. You fired a pistol. How do you plead to these charges?"

"Well, I did all that."

"Why did you disturb our airspace?"

"I did not have a donkey to ride here. The aircraft was the only means of transportation available to me. This means of transportation will not permanently damage your airspace. The aircraft moves through the air without harming the air." The interpreter giggled during its translation.

"Why did you not have a visa?"

"If I had requested a visa, I would have been shot."

"Why did you bring with you a pistol?"

"The pistol was a required part of my equipment; without it, I would not have been allowed to fly."

"Why did you fire the pistol?"

"To keep away people who I feared might damage something of great value to the rest of the world."

"Are you prepared to sign a confession admitting your guilt to these crimes?"

"If that is what you want."

"It is my judgment that this is a special case and no punishment is warranted. Do not fear. This will not interfere with your plans."

Having satisfied the requirements of the legal bureaucracy, the judge smiled, shook hands with Belenko, and asked the interpreter to wish him well.

During the judicial proceedings, a package and note had been delivered to his cell: "It was nice talking with you. I will be pleased if these books help you pass the time. With best regards, Jim."

The package contained two books: a collection of the works of Aleksandr Solzhenitsyn and *The Great Terror* by Robert Conquest, both in Russian. Anyone caught reading either in the Soviet Union could expect a minimum prison sentence of three years. Drawn by the lure of the forbidden, Belenko read curiously at first, then passionately, then as a man driven and possessed. He read through the day and into the night, and he trembled often as he read.

The words of Solzhenitsyn reeked and shouted of the truth, the truth he long had seen but the fundamental meaning of which he never had fully comprehended. He had seen the village Solzhenitsyn recreates in *Matryona's House*, the mean, hungry, desolate, cockroach-infested, manure-ridden, hopeless village. Although Solzhenitsyn was describing a village of the 1950s, Belenko had seen the same village in 1976; he had seen it at Chuguyevka; he had seen it at the village beyond the fence of the training center where he studied the MiG-25. He had seen the *zek* in *One Day in the Life of Ivan Denisovich.* He had seen him just last spring on the road from the freight terminal to Chuguyevka. In fact, the dying Ukrainian exile he had picked up had looked just like Ivan Denisovich.

The Great Terror unveiled for Belenko the full dimensions in all their horror of the Stalin purges, wherein at least 15 million people—children, women, men, Party faithful and heroes, loyal generals and intelligence officers, workers, peasants—were starved, shot, or tortured to death. Never had he read a book which so meticulously documented every stated fact by references to published sources, mostly Soviet sources, brilliantly collated to convey a message of overwhelming authenticity. All of Khrushchev's calumnies about Stalin were true, just as the millions or billions of deifying words previously uttered and printed about him were lies. But Khrushchev, Belenko now realized, had let loose only a little of the truth.

Caring for neither food nor drink, he read and reread well into the early morning of his third day until he was sure, sure that one quest of his life had ended in fulfillment.

All his intellectual life he had detected symptoms of a sickness in Soviet society, signs that something was fundamentally wrong. They proliferated, overpowered, and ultimately drove him away with the conclusion that the illness was incurable. Yet he never understood the underlying cause; he never discerned any logic or pattern in all the failures, stupidities, cruelties, and injustices he observed. Now Solzhenitsyn, a Russian studying Soviet society from within, and Conquest, an Englishman, analyzing it from without, independently and in separate ways gave him the understanding for which he always had quested.

The perennial shortages of virtually everything the people wanted and needed, the enduring backwardness and chronic failures of agriculture, the inefficiencies of the factories were not really the fault of individuals or local bureaucrats or Khrushchev or Stalin, as the official explanations variously claimed. Neither was the maintenance of a rigidly stratified society under the name of a classless society, tyranny under the banner of freedom, concentration camps under the label of justice. Even the ghastly pogroms ordered by Stalin and the ridiculous, ruinous economic policies of Khrushchev were only superficially their fault.

The cause of all lay within the Soviet system itself. Dependent for survival on tyranny, it inevitably spawned tyrants, gave them sway, and could tolerate within the body politic no antidote to their excesses or errors. During his twenty-nine years under the system, life always had been essentially the same because the system was the same. And whatever cosmetics might be applied to alter its appearance before the world, however repression might ebb and rise in intensity, the system always would yield essentially the same results.

If everything they said about communism, about themselves was a lie, then maybe what they said about the rest of the world also was a lie. Maybe there is hope. Anyway, I am free of it forever.

But by midmorning Belenko had cause to wonder whether he really was free of it. The bright young Foreign Office official who accompanied him from Hakodate came to the prison, and the concern manifested by his face and word caused Belenko concern.

"The Soviet Union is exerting enormous pressure on us. They do not believe that you are acting voluntarily. They are accusing us of keeping you by use of force and narcotics, and we have been put in a very difficult situation. They are trying desperately to take you back.

"Now you do not have to do this. It is entirely your

choice. But it would be a great service to Japan if you would meet with a Soviet representative and disprove their accusations, prove that you are acting out of your own desires."

"What will happen if I refuse?"

"We will advise the Russians that you have refused and continue to protect you until you leave for the States."

"All right. I do not want to do it, but I will do it."

"Thank you very much for your courage. I know how hard this will be for you. It also will be dangerous for you, and I want to make you aware of the dangers.

"They will try immediately to establish intimate psychological contact with you, to make you feel that you are lost and they have come to rescue you and take you home, where you belong. They will exploit your relatives and probably bring appealing letters and messages from them. They will try to dominate and control the conversation and confuse you.

"But you have the right to interrupt and say whatever you want. The meeting will be brief, as brief as you desire. You may leave whenever you wish. The main point is to prove that you are acting voluntarily. Just tell the truth.

"If you weaken and say you want to go back, we cannot help you. But if you adhere to your desires, we will stand by you. So will the Americans."

The Japanese that afternoon further revealed the gravity with which they anticipated the confrontation by taking Belenko into a conference room for a detailed rehearsal. They pointed to a table behind which the Soviet emissary would sit and another fifteen yards away where Belenko would sit. Three security guards would protect him, and one would stand on either side of the Russian. If he drew any kind of weapon or attempted to move toward Belenko, he would be struck down instantly. Again they stressed that he could depart at any time and pointed to the door through which he should leave whenever he wanted.

A big redheaded American, with a commanding presence, deep baritone voice, and a strong handshake, visited Belenko the next day, a couple of hours before the confrontation. Although he said nothing about the imminent meeting, his purpose probably was to reassure Belenko, and he succeeded.

"Tonight you fly to America. We have your tickets; all arrangements are made. You, of course, will not fly alone. Someone will be waiting for you at the plane. Is there anything I can do for you? Do you have any questions?"

"No questions. I am ready."

The waning afternoon sun cast a dim light and shadows from the trees rustling in the wind outside danced in the conference room as Belenko entered. A KGB officer, who posed as a first secretary of the Soviet Embassy in Tokyo, behaved just as the Japanese predicted, jumping up and starting his spiel before Belenko sat down.

"I am an official of the Soviet Embassy, and I want to tell you how much all your comrades sympathize with you. The Soviet government as well as everyone else knows that what happened was not your fault. We know that you did not voluntarily land your plane in Japan, that you lost your way and were forced down. We know that you are being held in a Japanese prison against your will and that the Japanese have drugged you with narcotics. But even if there were a mistake on your part, and we know there was not, but even if there were, I can assure you on the highest authority that it is forgiven; it is as nothing. I have come to help you home, back to your own people, to your loving wife and son, to your relatives. They have been able to do little but weep since your misfortune, and your adoring wife, Ludmilla, is inconsolable. Even your beautiful little son, Dmitri, young as he is, cries at life without his father.

"All your relatives, your wife, your father who served our Mother Country so heroically, your mother, your aunt, who was so kind to you as a child, have joined in sending a collective letter to you."

How could they get them together so quickly, from the Donbas, Siberia, the Far East? It's preposterous. And I don't care anyway.

As the KGB officer started to read the letter aloud, Belenko stood and looked him in the eyes with unflinching contempt. "Wait a minute," he interrupted. "I flew to Japan voluntarily and on purpose. I am here voluntarily and because of my own desires. Nobody has used force on me or given me any kind of drugs. I on my own initiative have requested political asylum in the United States. Excuse me. Our conversation is ended. I must leave."

"Traitor!" shouted the KGB officer. "You know what happens to traitors! One way or another we will get you back! We will get you back."

The Japanese official presiding over the meeting switched off the tape recorder and told the Russian, "You may leave."

Belenko stepped into the anteroom and unrestrained jubilation. The dozen or so Japanese gathered there cheered him, hugged him, slapped his back, and bumped into each other in eagerness to shake his hand. "You were magnificent; we are proud of you," said the Foreign Office official who had asked him to meet the Russian. "You will have a wonderful life in America. It is a great country made up of people from all over the world." Handing Belenko a bottle of Stolichnaya vodka, he said, "We would like you to take this with you to America as a present from your Japanese friends."

When I first saw them, I thought they were funny. Their talk sounded like the chirping of birds. In a way they are like Chechens. If you understand them, you see they are a remarkable people, very strong people. They have been so sincere and kind to me.

"No, I want to drink it now with my Japanese friends."

Paper cups were brought, and the Japanese manfully downed the vodka to which they were unaccustomed. Its intoxicating effects soon changed their grimaces to laughter, and they bade farewell to Belenko in high spirits. "Remember, you are always welcome back in Japan. And next time we will show you Tokyo."

They left the prison in darkness and drove to the airport in another heavily escorted motorcade; police swung open a gate, and the car sped across the runway to a Northwest Orient Airlines Boeing 747. Inside, Jim, the Embassy officer, led Belenko into the coach section, and nobody paid any particular attention to them. As they took off, Jim patted him on the shoulder. "You're on your way."

As Belenko had never seen a wide-bodied yet, its quietness and size amazed him, and he felt as if he were in an opulent theater. The number of flight attendants and their attentiveness to the passengers also surprised him.

After the 747 leveled off at 39,000 feet, Jim said, "Okay, let's go to our room." The first-class lounge on the upper deck was reserved exclusively for them and a huge, fierce-looking man whom the U.S. embassy officer introduced as a U.S. marine. The captain admitted Belenko to the flight deck and for nearly an hour, with Jim interpreting, answered his questions about the 747, its equipment and life as a commercial pilot. Belenko simply did not believe that only three men could manage such an enormous plane, though they carefully showed and explained how they could.

The rest of the crew is hidden somewhere. But if it's their job to fool me and impress me, I'll let them think they've succeeded.

Neither did he believe that the dinner—caviar, smoked salmon, smoked trout, soup, salad, filet mignon, potato balls, asparagus, fruit and cheese, strawberries and ice cream, white wine, red wine, champagne—was normal first-class fare on an international flight.

They are just putting on a show for me, no matter what Jim says.

However, he did believe and was moved by the stewardesses who after dinner came singly or in pairs to speak briefly to him.

"We are proud to have you aboard Northwest and in our country."

"I want to congratulate you. You have done a great thing."

"You are very brave. I am proud to meet you."

One stewardess, a pretty, freckle-faced pixie, had no words. She only took off her stewardess' wings, pinned them on him, and kissed him on the cheek.

Belenko kept wondering when the Dark Forces in the person of Jim would begin his interrogation, until Jim made clear there would be none. "You must be utterly exhausted, so just relax and sleep as much as you can. You have nothing to worry about. Your first problem will be to learn English. But you'll master it quickly, and you'll have an accent which all the girls will think is cute. You have a great future ahead of you. You'll see."

After the lounge lights dimmed and Jim, though not the marine, dozed off, Belenko thought not of the future but of the past. Had he done right in fleeing? Had he done right in refusing to go back? Would his relatives be better off if he returned? Who would suffer? He tried, as was his wont, to analyze and answer logically.

Even if they did not punish me, and they would punish me, but even if they did not, what could I do back there to change things? I could do nothing. Can I do anything in the West? I don't know. Maybe. Could I help my relatives? If I could not help them, if I could not have good relations with them before, why now? Will they be hurt? Not my father, my mother, my aunt. The KGB will find I have not seen them for years. Ludmilla and Dmitri? No; her parents have enough influence to protect them. Who then? The Monster and his superiors; the political officers; the KGB. Well, they deserve it. No. No matter what happens I have done right. I do not want to live anymore unless I am free.

Despite the certitude of his conclusion, an amorphous malaise troubled him.

All right, what's your trouble now?

Reviewing and ordering his recollections, he isolated and identified the cause. It was the echo of harshly shouted words: "One way or another we will get you back."

Lt. Viktor Belenko's Soviet MiG-25 jet interceptor at Hakodate Airport in northern Japan on September 6, 1976. Japanese security officers guard the partly covered super-secret aircraft, which has slid to a halt after overshooting the runway. (*ASAHI SHIMBUN PHOTO*)

Belenko's MiG-25 "Foxbat" is covered by Japanese officials after its surprise landing. The skid marks made as it shot off the runway can be seen at upper right. (*AP WIREPHOTO*)

Japanese officials examine the cockpit of Belenko's MiG-25 on September 7. Their inspection proceeded cautiously because of fears that the plane was booby-trapped. (*KYODO NEWS SERVICE PHOTO*)

Viktor Belenko covers himself with a jacket as he is led by security men in Tokyo on September 7, after having been flown from Hokkaido earlier in the day. (*AP WIREPHOTO*)

The Soviet MiG-25 "Foxbat" resting at the end of the field of Hakodate Airport. In this picture, dated September 6, the super-secret aircraft is uncovered. (*AP WIREPHOTO*)

Japanese military officials investigating the MiG-25 at Hakodate Airport on September 12. A temporary shield has been constructed around the airplane. (*ASAHI SHIMBUN PHOTO*)

The photograph of Viktor Belenko, taken earlier in the year, released by Soviet officials. (*UPI*)

Belenko, with a Japanese security officer, leaves for the Tokyo airport to fly to America and "the lair of the Dark Forces."

Plainclothed U.S. Air Force experts carry machinery and tools into Hakodate Airport on September 19 at the start of a joint U.S.-Japanese investigation of the MiG-25. The team disassembled the aircraft to uncover Soviet secrets long coveted by the West. (*ASAHI SHIMBUN PHOTO*)

The MiG-25, its wings removed, is loaded onto a USAF C-5A transport to be airlifted on September 25 to a base in central Japan for further study. The banner says: "Sayonara, people of Hakodate, sorry for the trouble." (*ASAHI SHIMBUN PHOTO*)

Belenko, in wig and sunglasses, and American escort at Los Angeles International Airport after arriving from Japan. The attempt to confuse newsmen led the picture to be captioned: *"Which One Is the Real Soviet Pilot?"* (*AP WIREPHOTO*)

Disassembled and packed, the MiG-25 is loaded onto a Russian ship at Hitachi port on November 12, 67 days after Belenko flew the super-secret jet to Hakodate Airport. (*KYODO NEWS SERVICE PHOTO*)

"We Will Get You Back"

Viktor Ivanovich Belenko was one defector the Russians were determined to get back. Embarrassing or damaging as defections by artists, intellectuals, diplomats, or KGB officers may be, all, after a fashion, can be explained away to the world and the Soviet people. It is not too difficult for Soviet propaganda organs and the KGB disinformation department to portray an artist or intellectual as an egotistical eccentric or a spoiled degenerate leaning toward lunacy. It is not surprising if an occasional diplomat, having lived and worked in the rottenness of the West, succumbs to that rottenness and sinks into alcoholism, embezzlement, or insanity. And KGB officers? Who gives a damn about them anyway? They spend their lives selling the Soviet people, and each other, and a few are bound to wind up selling themselves.

But Belenko, symbolically and actually, was different—a son of the working class; a toiler in the fields and factories; an elite officer, whose record was strewn with commendations; a pure product of the Party; the quintessence of the New Communist Man. As a Soviet journalist said to Washington *Post* correspondent Peter Osnos in Moscow, "This was one of our very best people, a pilot in the air force entrusted to fly a top secret plane." To admit that Belenko was less than the best would be to admit that the Party had been terribly, ludicrously wrong, that the very concept of the New Communist Man might be a myth. Thus, Belenko became probably the only defector in Soviet history about whom the Soviet Union had only good to say.

Were Belenko to remain alive and at liberty abroad, dangerous thoughts and precedents would arise in the minds of the people in general and other pilots in particular. If you cannot trust someone so perfect as Belenko, whom can you trust? Who is loyal? The question was reflected in a joke that spread through Moscow immediately after the British Broadcasting Corporation reported the sensational news of the escape: "Did you hear? From now on they are going to train only Politburo members to fly those planes." And other pilots inevitably would ask themselves, "If Belenko can do it, why can't I?" There were additional perils. Belenko was probably the most knowledgeable military man to flee since World War II, and the secrets and insights he could impart to the Americans would harm the Soviet Union. But worse, should he elect to speak out publicly, especially to the Soviet people, his words could be even more devastating than the loss of secrets.

The whole situation could be retrieved if Belenko were enticed back or if the Japanese or Americans were intimidated, duped, or cajoled into delivering him. After appropriate treatment and conditioning in a KGB psychiatric ward, he could be paraded forth as proof of the perfidies of the West, a true Soviet hero who had slipped out of the snares of the Dark Forces and come home to the Mother Country to attest to their perfidies. His staged appearances, the lines he mouthed, would dramatize to all pilots and everybody else the futility of trying to get away.

Thus, within an hour after Belenko and the MiG-25 had plowed off the runway in Hakodate, the Soviet Union initiated a massive, unprecedented campaign to recover him. In the Crisis Rooms of Washington the men who watched and participated in the intensifying international struggle that followed appreciated how great the stakes were.

Steven Steiner, thirty-six, Yale '63, Columbia Graduate School '66, slept from noon to eight on Sunday, September 5. He missed a balmy, sunny afternoon and upon awakening regretted anew that he could not take his wife and three children for an outing on that delightful Labor Day weekend. But he had the duty as Senior Watch Officer at the State Department Operations Center beginning at 12:01 A.M. Monday, and his family, having been with him at diplomatic posts in Yugoslavia and Moscow, had adjusted to the inconvenient hours he sometimes had to work. Just the night before he had worked the same shift.

Dressed in blue jeans, a sports shirt, and loafers, Steiner entered the Watch Center located in Room 7516 of the State Department at 11:15 P.M. and put his yogurt and diet cola in the refrigerator for later. He came early because he was required to read all the recent cables and be briefed about the world situation by the outgoing Senior Watch Officer before assuming responsibility for the Watch. Secretary of State Henry Kissinger was traveling in Europe, and the Operations Center is the Secretary's twenty-four-hour link to Washington. So he anticipated a heavy flow of messages and a busy night.

Steiner noted in the log at 12:01 A.M. that he had taken over the Watch and made his second entry at 12:47, recording that the Watch team had obtained and cabled information concerning Africa requested by Kissinger's entourage in Zurich.

At 1:35 A.M. the special closed-circuit telephone rang in the Watch Center—a "NOIWON" (National Operations and Intelligence Watch Officers Network) alert signaling the entire U.S. crisis-management community that something extraordinary had occurred. As Steiner picked up his phone, other Watch Officers lifted similar emergency phones at the Situation Room in the White House, the National Military Command Center at the Pentagon, the Operations Centers at the Central Intelligence Agency in Langley, Virginia, and the National Security Agency in Fort Meade, Maryland. A male voice announced over the circuit: "The Defense Intelligence Agency is convening a NOIWON alert. On the basis of a preliminary report from the U.S. Fifth Air Force, we understand that a Soviet MiG-25 has landed at Hakodate in northern Japan. . . ." The MiG had touched down at 12:50 A.M. Washington time. The circumstances of the flight and intent of the pilot had not yet been ascertained by American representatives in Japan. Two more alerts from the DIA at 1:49 and 2:06 added a few sparse details but failed to clarify whether the pilot had landed intentionally or of necessity. Meanwhile, the news ticker in the Watch Center typed out an Agence France-Presse dispatch reporting that the pilot had jumped from the aircraft and commenced firing a pistol. To Steiner, that sounded as though the Soviet pilot probably had lost his way or been forced down by mechanical trouble and was hostile to the West.

But at 4:30 A.M. the NOIWON bell rang a fourth time, and the voice speaking from the Pentagon was excited. The Soviet pilot, Viktor I. Belenko, had told representatives of the Japanese Foreign Ministry that he had flown the MiG purposely to Japan and desired political asylum in the United States.

At the National Military Command Center someone shouted, "Goddamn! We've got a Foxbat [NATO designation of the MiG-25] and the pilot to boot. Goddamn!"

With this the situation became all the more serious and urgent, especially so because of one of the most shameful incidents of pusillanimity in American history. On November 23, 1970 Seaman Simas Kudirka jumped from a Soviet fishing ship onto a U.S. Coast Guard cutter while the two ships were tied up alongside one another in American territorial waters off Martha's Vineyard. Ashore in Boston, a Coast Guard rear admiral, acting in what he presumed to be the spirit of détente, ordered officers on the cutter to hand the defector back to the Russians. Contrary to U.S. naval and political traditions, the American officers allowed six Russians to board the cutter, beat the defector and drag him back to the Soviet ship.

As a consequence of this disgrace, the U.S. government adopted measures to ensure that no bona fide Soviet defector ever again would be turned away or that, if he were, those responsible would have their professional heads chopped off. Precise instructions were promulgated to be followed from the moment it appeared that a foreign national was seeking political asylum. These included a stringent requirement that all American officials who might be concerned be swiftly notified and that a formal, permanent record of everyone involved be maintained.

Accordingly, Steiner and his Watch team successively and rapidly telephoned at their homes and awakened an aide to State Department Counselor Helmut Sonnenfeldt, Director of Press Relations Frederick Brown, and officials in the Bureau of East Asian Affairs, the Soviet and Japanese Desks, the Humanitarian Affairs Bureau, the Visa Office, and the Immigration and Naturalization Service. A full report was cabled to Kissinger. Then Steiner on his own initiative telephoned the U.S. Embassy in Tokyo because from his service in Moscow, he recognized the gravity and potential danger involved. Please emphasize to our Japanese friends, he said, that the physical safety of the pilot is paramount. Probably they already realize that. But it cannot be stressed too much. Protect the pilot. Be sure he is free to make his own decision.

By 6:00 A.M. the Watch Center was crowded with men and women called out of their sleep to study the messages flooding in from the Embassy, the Pentagon, the CIA, the Fifth Air Force in Japan, and the wire services. On a typically active night, the Watch Officer's log entries noting major events might fill one page; Steiner's had filled four. Having had no time for his yogurt and cola, he drove home through calm, treelined streets, tired and pleased: pleased that he and the Watch team had done their duty, pleased that people in other agencies had done their duty, that the system had worked exactly as it was supposed to work.

In Paris, reporters accosted Kissinger and peppered him with questions about the fate of Belenko. "The United States will probably grant asylum," he said. "If we do not, you may assume I have been overruled."

Actually, once Belenko put his request for asylum in writing, there was no question about American willingness to accept him. The Director of Central Intelligence in consultation with the Attorney General and the Commissioner of Immigration is empowered, without reference to immigration laws or any other laws, to admit up to 100 aliens to the United States annually. But in this case the decision was made instantly by President Ford himself.

He learned of Belenko's flight before breakfast. His national security adviser, Lieutenant General Brent Scowcroft, recalls that the President at once comprehended the import of Belenko's flight, and was extremely interested.

What did appear in question that Labor Day morning was the outcome of the ferocious Soviet pressures to browbeat and intimidate the Japanese into surrendering Belenko and the MiG-25.

Promptly after Belenko landed, the Soviet Embassy in Tokyo announced that the Soviet Union possessed "an inviolable right to protect its military secrets." The MiG-25 was a secret military aircraft. Therefore, the Japanese must return it immediately and permit no one to look at it. The embassy further declared, as if addressing some Soviet colony, that the granting of asylum to Belenko "could not be tolerated." The Soviet government lodged repeated protests demanding the immediate return of Belenko and the plane. One was so brazenly and harshly worded that the Japanese characterized it as unparalleled in the history of diplomatic relations with the USSR.

Soviet aircraft swarmed around Japan in a deliberate and insulting display of power. At sea, Soviet naval vessels started seizing Japanese fishing craft and hauling their crews off to Soviet prisons. These blatant piratical depredations were meant to make the Japanese cower by showing them how the Russians could disrupt the fishing industry on which their island economy heavily depends.

Meanwhile, the Russians tried to get at the plane directly. Late in the afternoon of the sixth, a Russian using a false name showed up at the Hakodate Airport administrator's office, identifying himself as "a crewman of a Soviet merchant ship being repaired at Hakodate harbor." He said he had come to interview his compatriot Belenko. A Japanese official stonily turned him away.

The next afternoon three more Russians knocked at the airport administration office. Their spokesman introduced himself as the "Tass bureau chief in Tokyo" and his two companions as "Aeroflot engineers."

"It's our job to ship the airplane out, but we understand that its landing gear is damaged," he said earnestly. "We must have the parts to repair them and would like to ascertain how badly the gear is smashed. So we would like to go on out to the plane, look around, and take some photographs."

Airport administrator Masao Kageoka smiled politely. "Well, the plane is now under control of the Japanese police, and it is beyond my authority to grant you access. By the way, I don't quite understand in which capacity you are here."

"Oh," said the "Tass" man, "I'm here as a civilian."

This same indefatigable intelligence officer visited the regional headquarters of the Hokkaido police the next morning and announced that he was reporting for his "briefing" on the plane and pilot. The police said, "We can't give you any details. Get out!"

On Tuesday, September 7, the White House announced that President Ford himself had decided to grant Belenko asylum in the United States. "If he asks for asylum here, he will be welcome," said Press Secretary Ron Nessen. Unfortunately, some misconstrued the phrasing to mean that Belenko had not yet asked for asylum.

But, as an official statement issued at the same time by

the State Department made clear, there was no doubt about Belenko's desires: "The Japanese government notified us of the pilot's request for asylum, and they did it yesterday. We have informed the government of Japan that we are prepared to allow the pilot to come to the United States. We understand that is his desire. I believe the same comment or a comment to that effect was made this morning at the White House."

The announcements in Washington, coupled with indications emerging from a Japanese Cabinet meeting that Belenko was about to be transferred to the Americans, incited the Russians to new fury and desperation. Soviet Ambassador Dmitri Polyansky read to the Japanese Deputy Foreign Minister a statement, the crudity of which exceeded all bounds of conventional diplomatic propriety. The Russians declared that Belenko had made an emergency landing and accused the Japanese of lying about it, or "fabricating a story" to conceal the "physical violence and other unforgivable means" employed to kidnap him.

After the confrontation between Belenko and the KGB officer, Soviet Embassy spokesman Aleksandr Shishaev denounced the meeting as "a farce, a shame on the Japanese government." He claimed that "it was impossible for him [Belenko] to answer questions. He was under the influence of narcotics. He sat there like a dummy."

With the departure of Belenko for the United States, the Soviet pressures on Japan did not abate; they merely were refocused on recovery of the MiG-25 before the Americans could study it. Surveillance flights by Soviet fighters and seizure of Japanese fishing craft and their crews at sea continued. Moscow threatened economic retaliation and hinted at all sorts of dire, though unspecified, consequences unless the Japanese bowed at once.

A flurry of secret messages about the MiG-25 bounced back and forth between Tokyo and Washington, many handled through General Scowcroft, who coordinated and mediated between the Defense and State departments. The Pentagon wanted to bring the plane to the United States, test it, fly it, keep it. "Absolutely," remembers Donald Rumsfeld, then Secretary of Defense. "We wanted the plane. We wanted metal samples; to fly it, take it apart, then fly it again."

Some in the State Department, however, were skittish, fearing that retention of the MiG would strain détente and complicate other relations with the Russians. And the State Department was reluctant to pressure the Japanese, who initially were inclined to manage disposition of the plane in a manner that would spare the Soviet Union as much embarrassment as possible.

Out of all the bureaucratic wrangling, a compromise emerged. How long would scientists, engineers, and technicians require to extract all data desired by disassembling and studying the plane on the ground? A minimum of thirty days, the Pentagon said.

The Japanese promptly pledged to make the MiG-25 available at least that long, provided American specialists wore civilian clothes and acted as consultants working under their supervision.

In their threats, insolence, and condescension, the Russians had gone too far and provoked the Japanese government, with widespread support of the citizenry, into a posture of defiance. The Japanese now started subtly taunting the Russians. Rejecting all Soviet protests and charges, the government expressed surprise that the Soviet Union had yet to apologize for violating Japanese airspace. Said Foreign Minister Kiichi Miyazawa: "I realize the Soviet Union is the kind of nation that gets bogged down in red tape in making declarations, but at the very least, the Soviet Union has a duty to control the actions of its uniformed military men. It's like landing in a neighbor's garden and not even bothering to say 'Boo.' "

As for all the strident Soviet demands that the MiG-25 be given back, another Foreign Ministry official said, "The Soviet Union should first explain what it thinks of the incident. It is no way for anyone to try to take back something he has thrown, even though inadvertently, into the yard of his neighbor."

What then will happen to the plane? Well, the Japanese solemnly explained, that is a complicated issue. There are precedents for returning it and precedents for keeping it. We will just have to see. But for the time being, we will have to retain it as "evidence" while our investigation of the whole matter continues.

The Los Angeles *Times* summed up the situation in a brief editorial:

> The trouble with the Soviet authorities is that they just won't *listen*. There they are, kicking, screaming and all but turning blue in the face while they demand the immediate return of their highly sophisticated and very secret MiG-25 jet fighter, flown to Japan by a defecting Russian pilot. And there's the Japanese foreign minister, trying calmly, and with impeccable legal logic, to explain that the plane can't be returned now because it's evidence in a crime, the crime being the violation of Japanese airspace by said Russian pilot, whose punishment—and let no one say he didn't ask for it—is likely to be a one-way ticket to the United States.
>
> Material evidence in a crime such as this plainly deserves the most careful going-over, perhaps even by experts from several countries. After all, who knows what that pilot could have been surreptitiously carrying? Perhaps a little caviar hidden among the plane's electronic countermeasures? Maybe a liter of vodka secreted somewhere in the airframe? A hot balalaika or two cached in the turbojet engines? The only way to find out is to take the plane apart piece by piece, as the cops did with the smuggler's car in "The French Connection."
>
> The interests of the law must, of course, be served. It all seems very sensible and straightforward to us. Why the Russians can't understand is a puzzle.

With the revelation that American "consultants" were en route to assist in the Japanese "investigation," the Russians realized they had no chance now of preventing examination and exploitation of the MiG-25. So they redirected their propaganda toward the Soviet people and their pressures toward the United States.

Tass on September 14 initiated the Soviet efforts to represent Belenko as a hero and patriot abducted and spirited away against his will by the Dark Forces with the connivance of the devious and unscrupulous Japanese. According to Tass, Belenko during a routine training flight strayed off course, ran out of fuel, and made a forced landing at Hakodate. (An unidentified Soviet source attempted to lend credence to this version by telling Western newsmen that Belenko maintained radio contact with his base up until his landing.) Tass asserted that Japanese police clamped a hood over Belenko's head, dragged him away by his arms, shoved him into a car, and hid him in isolation, refusing Soviet pleas to see him.

On the very day following the landing of the Soviet aircraft in Japan, an official representative of the White House announced that President Ford had decided to grant asylum to the Soviet pilot. This same White House representative was forced to acknowledge that the American authorities did not even know whether the pilot had sought asylum in the U.S.

It is difficult to label this announcement as anything but inflammatory. Even the sensation-oriented American press and television called this 'unusual' for the White House, apparently dictated by reason of the election campaign. It is evident that American "special services" were behind this "invitation" to the Soviet pilot. Subsequent events showed their participation in the removal of Belenko to the U.S. . . .

Despite persistent demands on the part of the Soviets, Japanese authorities refused for several days to satisfy the appeal for a meeting between Soviet representatives and the pilot. When such a meeting finally took place, it was reduced to a worthless farce. At a distance of 25– 30 meters, fenced off from the representatives of the Soviet Embassy in Japan by a barricade of office tables, sat Belenko, like a mannequin, surrounded by police and other representatives of the Japanese authorities. Not even a Soviet doctor, who would have been able to render a professional opinion as to the physical condition of the pilot, was allowed at the meeting.

This was in no way a meeting conducive to talking with Belenko. His two or three incoherent sentences were hardly confirmation of the Japanese representatives' assertions as to the pilot's intention "to receive political asylum" in the U.S. The entire course of the meeting, which lasted only seven minutes in all, including time to translate his sentences into Japanese, demonstrated that Belenko was in an abnormal condition, under the influence of drugs or something else. Immediately following this meeting, he was placed in an airplane owned by an American company and taken, under guard, to the U.S. This is how the Japanese authorities, in collaboration with American "special services," treated the Soviet pilot.

Foreign Minister Andrei Gromyko flew to New York on September 20 and, when asked about the Belenko affair, said, "This is a matter that will come up in discussions between us and the United States." That evening during a private dinner with Kissinger at the Waldorf-Astoria, Gromyko emphasized that the return of Belenko was an issue of such grave importance to the Soviet Union that Brezhnev himself was personally concerned with it.

The Russians, he said, were not at all sure that the man presented to them in Tokyo was even Belenko. The belief that Belenko had been abducted and was being held against his will would continue to poison U.S.-Soviet relations until it was eliminated, and it could be extirpated only if the Russians, with one of their own physicians present, were allowed to talk personally to Belenko at length.

In Washington the Soviets, who sometimes try to lobby in Congress as assiduously as the AFL-CIO or American Medical

Association, sought to generate pressures in Congress for the return of Belenko. An emissary from the Soviet Embassy delivered a handwritten letter from Belenko's wife, Ludmilla, and mother to the office of Representative Dante Fascell, chairman of the U.S. commission that monitors compliance with the Helsinki Accords, especially the human rights provisions. The Russian handwriting was that of Belenko's wife; the maudlin words almost certainly were those of the KGB. They appealed to the congressman to uphold his commitment to human rights by helping to free this captured son and husband and reunite him with his loving, grief-stricken family. And repeatedly, the Embassy dispatched its second ranking member, Yuly Vorontsov, one of the Soviet Union's three or four most forceful diplomatic operatives, to demand from the State Department an opportunity to confront, or rather, to have a long, leisurely talk with, Belenko.

In Moscow the Foreign Ministry staged a melodramatic conference for the foreign and Soviet press corps, starring Belenko's wife and his mother, whom he had last seen twenty-seven years before, when he was two years old. Foreign Ministry official Lev Krylov, who presided over the show, declared at the outset that "Western propaganda" stories that Belenko had voluntarily flown to Japan because of dissatisfaction with life in the Soviet Union were malicious fabrications. "All this is a lie from beginning to end."

Ludmilla spoke emotionally and often wept before the cameras. "We do not believe and will never believe that he is voluntarily abroad. I do not doubt Viktor's love and loyalty. And this gives me the absolute right to declare that something terrible has happened to Viktor and that he needs assistance, which I request all of you present here to give him.

"On Sunday, one day before the terrible event, Viktor spent the entire day walking and playing with our son, as he usually did on his free days. They worked figurines out of plastic and read fairy stories. I baked pies, and Viktor helped me do it. We had supper in the evening and went to bed. Before going to sleep, Viktor reminded me that our friend's birthday was several days away and proposed that we give him several crystal glasses at his birthday party. On the morning of September sixth, he told me he would be back early from the flight and would take our son from kindergarten. He kissed me and Dima and went off, as he did every day.

"Nothing bode us ill. I am sure that something happened during the flight, and he was forced to land the plane on foreign territory. I firmly believe that Viktor was and will continue to be a Soviet man. It was his dream to be a test pilot. On September third, actually three days before the incident, he sent the necessary papers for appointment as test pilot to the command.

"Western press reports that my husband requested political asylum in the U.S.A. are a deliberate lie. I am absolutely sure that such a statement was fabricated against his will.

"Our family is well-off. We live in a good apartment with every convenience. My husband is well paid. His ability as a flier was highly appreciated by the commanding officers. He is a patriot. He received only commendations during his service. He had excellent marks in school. We have no news from Viktor to this day. Is this not testimony that he is under coercion?"

Pausing to sob now and then, Ludmilla read excerpts from a letter she had sent to her beloved kidnapped husband. "Darling, I am convinced that some incredible misfortune happened to you. . . . My dear Viktor, we are waiting for you at home; return soon. I was officially reassured at the highest level here that you will be forgiven, even if you have made a mistake. . . . Take all steps and ensure your return to the homeland." Tearfully, Ludmilla told the press that in the name of humanity she had addressed a personal appeal to President Ford and quoted further from her letter to Belenko: "I rely on [Ford's] humaneness. Though this is a personal matter for us, he is also a father and must understand our sorrow; help me, you, and our son to be together."

The performance of Belenko's mother, suddenly lifted out of obscurity in the Caucasus, flown to Moscow, handsomely dressed, coiffured, and drilled, was good, if brief, considering that she personally knew nothing of the man she had last seen as a child of two. She did not cry as well as Ludmilla, but did produce some tears, which she dabbed with a white handkerchief. Her few lines were aimed at mothers everywhere,* but most important, at Soviet mothers.

"My son, Viktor, has always been a patriot. In the family and his service, he was single-minded and level-headed. I am convinced that some misfortune happened to him. And I, as mother, am deeply pained that someone wants to take advantage of my son's trouble, to prevent him from returning home. Who but a mother knows her child best? That is why I say that my Viktor is honest before the homeland and myself."

Krylov concluded the conference with another recitation of the infamous "arbitrary actions and lawlessness" of the devious Japanese and a denunciation of President Ford. Belenko's behavior in Japan proved that his flight was not intentional. "How else is one to explain his warning shots when unauthorized persons tried to approach the plane and his protests against the plane being photographed? The Japanese authorities used force on Belenko. He was handcuffed and had a bag over his head and was hidden on the back seat of a car when he was moved. . . ."

The combined American-Japanese abduction of Belenko, Krylov charged, was the act of callous homewreckers and flagrantly violated the Helsinki Accords on human rights only recently signed by President Ford himself.

The authors of the script the two ladies acted out understandably made a few factual errors, knowingly and unknowingly. Ludmilla never baked pies. Belenko never kissed his wife and son good-bye in the morning because he had to leave for the base so early that they were still asleep. He did not promise to pick up the child from kindergarten in midafternoon because, no matter when flights were completed, Shevsov or the Monster required all officers to remain on the base until 6:00 P.M. Like many fighter pilots, Belenko would have liked to become a test pilot. But he and the rest knew that, the right connections in Moscow being absent, such an aspiration was impossible of fulfillment, and he had never applied to be a test pilot.

Yet the appearance of the women, highly publicized in the Soviet Union, served the purpose of saving face for the Party. The faith of the Party in Belenko was not misplaced; the theories the Party followed in making of him a New Communist Man, a "Soviet man," as Ludmilla put it, were not invalid; none of the causes of the whole tragic incident were to be found within the Soviet system or the Mother Country. The trouble, as so many other Soviet troubles, grew out of the plotting of the Dark Forces.

However, the press conference did not produce the desired effects abroad. A succinct editorial in the Baltimore *Sun* typified much of the Western reaction:

> Soviet officialdom is not noted for humor except, on occasion, for the crude and inadvertent kind. A classic example of the latter must be credited to one Lev V. Krylov, a Foreign Ministry official assigned to orchestrate a campaign for the repatriation of Senior Lieutenant Viktor Belenko. Lieutenant Belenko is the Soviet pilot who defected to Japan September 6 in a MiG-25 that has been fondly scrutinized by American intelligence. The Kremlin wants Lieutenant Belenko back—not to punish, heaven forbid, but to reunite him with a wife and mother who wept in front of Soviet cameras. Comrade Krylov apparently was so affected by this display of emotion that he accused Japan and the United States of acts "tantamount to splitting a family by force."
>
> This would almost be funny if one could put out of mind, for a moment, the tens of thousands of German families divided by the Berlin Wall and the thousands of Russian Jews in exile who wait and wait and wait for the Soviet Union to grant exit permits to their relatives.

The renewed slander of Japan disseminated at the press conference, together with another incident, infuriated the

Japanese. In New York Gromyko summoned the new Japanese Foreign Minister, Zentaro Kosaka, to a Soviet UN office and, "offering not even a glass of water," spoke to him with such condescension that Kosaka, a courtly diplomat given to understatement, described the meeting as "extremely severe."

The Japanese government in Tokyo made public a specific rebuttal of the Soviet charges:

> The Soviets claim that a bag had been thrown over Lieutenant Belenko's head, but the fact was that he had his jacket thrown over his face by his expressed wish because he didn't want to be exposed to cameras.
> The Soviets claim that he was handcuffed because of the string seen in a picture of him, but the fact was that he held a paper bag containing his belongings, and the string of the bag appeared in the photo.
> The Soviets claim that he was kept 25–30 meters away from a Soviet Embassy official who came to see him, and the Japanese police interfered with the conversation. The fact was that the distance was only eight meters, and there was no interference whatever.
> The statement written and signed by Lieutenant Belenko was penned in a hotel in Hokkaido, where he landed the MiG-25 Foxbat. It was shown to Ambassador Dmitri Polyansky, but he refused to take it.
> [The statement said] "I hereby state that I, Viktor Ivanovich Belenko, do not wish to return to the Soviet Union and hope to reside in the United States. This decision has been made autonomously and out of my own free will. Viktor I. Belenko."

Privately the Japanese now said in effect to the Americans: Let's get started. We'll take it apart and ship it back to them in pieces.

On October 1 at four in the afternoon, President Ford received Gromyko and Soviet Ambassador Anatoly Dobrynin in the Oval Office of the White House. The subject of Belenko was not on the scheduled agenda of discussions, and Ford was surprised when Gromyko broached it—suddenly, indignantly, belligerently.

"We were after that plane like a dog in heat," he announced—not because the Russians cared about the loss of secrets it embodied *but because it was stolen.* Gromyko declared that Belenko was a thief, a common criminal whom the United States was obligated to extradite in the interests of simple justice. As a criminal, who had absconded with something as valuable as an aircraft, he obviously did not qualify for political asylum. Both international law and the interests of Soviet-American relations required that he be forcibly repatriated to face the prosecution his crime deserved.

President Ford made no attempt to disguise his astonishment or anger. Having been continuously briefed all along about Belenko and attendant developments, he was aware of the press conference in Moscow three days before and the consistent Soviet portrayal of Belenko as a "good man," a "Soviet man," a "patriot," "one of our best people," a highly commended officer, who, after straying off course, had been kidnapped and dragged away from country and family against his will, an esteemed comrade, who, even if he had made some unknown mistake, would be forgiven. Now, with a straight face, the foreign minister of the Soviet Union told him that this same man was a thief who must be brought before the bar of justice.

Ford was blunt. He was thoroughly familiar with the Belenko case. If ever there was an authentic Soviet defector, if ever anyone merited political asylum, it was Belenko. He was more than welcome in the United States as long as he lived. So far as the United States government was concerned, the issue was closed and not subject to further discussion or negotiation.

Through the decades the Russians have perfected to an art the practice of wresting concessions from other nations by thrashing about, growling menacingly, and acting like a great, frightening, unruly, and unpredictable bear. The reaction of the world often has been akin to that of indulgent parents undertaking to appease a spoiled child in the midst of a temper tantrum.

The Soviet temper tantrum had failed to wrest Belenko from the Japanese or the Americans. Now the only possibility lay in reaching him personally through words or other means.

With the Dark Forces

Flying toward what he envisioned as the very lair of the Dark Forces, Belenko knew little of the international storm he was precipitating and nothing about the intensity of continuing Soviet efforts to snare him. In his psychological approach to America, he was continuing the same intellectual quest which had driven him much of his life. He had to understand the underlying order, causes, purpose of the world he was entering. His reasoning convinced him that not all that the communists said about the United States could be true; analysis of their own words suggested the possibility that freedom of some kind actually might exist. But he was so inured to lies, deceit, hypocrisy, and the devious that he was skeptical of everything. For him, not even seeing was believing. Indeed, at times, the more obvious something seemed, the greater the cause in his mind to suspect the ulterior.

As the 747 descended toward Los Angeles, Jim handed him a wig and dark glasses so that he could not be recognized subsequently from pictures photographers might snap at the airport. On the runway they jumped into one of several waiting CIA cars and, escorted by police on motorcycles, darted through night traffic to a private airport, where a small passenger jet was ready to take off. Climbing into the plane, Belenko pulled off the wig, which was insufferably hot, and put away the glasses, drastically changing his appearance. One of the CIA men already in the plane looked around and, not seeing the man who came aboard as Belenko, panicked. "Jesus Christ! We've lost him already! Where in the hell did he go?"

Once Jim translated the exclamations, Belenko laughed along with the four CIA officers who were to accompany them, and all welcomed him in Russian. Belenko asked if they had any urgent questions, and the senior American replied much as Jim had over the Pacific: Relax; don't worry. There will be plenty of time to talk later. You're too tired now.

He was right. Days of tension, drama, anxiety, and time changes had drained him physically, intellectually, and emotionally. His impressions, sensations, and thoughts were blurred and imprecise, and he felt as if he were suspended midway in half-light between dream and reality.

The executive jet was to him a masterpiece of design, maneuvering as nimbly as a fighter while outfitted inside like an elegant hotel suite. *Well, I knew they were rich and built good airplanes.*

He sampled sandwiches set out on a table unfolded in the middle of the cabin—thick layers of turkey, corned beef, pastrami, cheese and lettuce and tomatoes, between slices of white, brown, and rye bread. He unhesitatingly requested instructions as to how to eat the sandwiches and wanted to know the contents of each. *They're delicious. But they probably have good food in the KGB, too. And so what? I didn't come here for food.*

There was something wrong with the CIA officers; at least something he expected was missing. In their late thirties or early forties, they looked too trim, too healthy; they were too neatly and, he thought, too expensively dressed; more troublesome, they were too much at ease, too casual, too friendly with each other and him, too, well, too open, too guileless. They wouldn't frighten anybody. *But of course.*

They're not typical. They were picked for this. We know the Dark Forces are clever. This is their way of fooling me.

Over the western deserts and the Rockies, Belenko slept in what he was told, but did not believe, was the CIA director's bunk. He was served tea upon awakening, and an officer pointed to the lights of a sprawling city on the port side of the plane. "That's Chicago. It's famous for stockyards and gangsters."

"Yes, the gangsters of Chicago are very famous in my country."

"Which country do you mean?"

Belenko grinned. "I understand your point."

They landed at Dulles Airport around 4:00 A.M. in darkness and heavy rain and drove for about an hour along back roads until the car turned into a long driveway. The headlights illuminated an imposing southern mansion built of red brick with tall windows, a double door, and a two-story veranda buttressed by white porticoes. Jim pointed to a bedroom and told him to sleep as long as he could. On the ceiling above the large bed, he spotted a fixture, either an air-conditioning outlet or a smoke detector. He was sure it was a concealed television camera continuously focused upon him, but he was too exhausted to care.

Belenko awakened at midmorning startled. *What's that nigger doing in my room?* Although he had never seen a black person, the prejudices against blacks he had been taught and absorbed throughout his life were thoroughly ingrained. On a scale of ten, blacks ranked in his eyes tenth, below Asian minorities of the Soviet population, below Jews. He warily eyed the middle-aged maid, who smiled at him, said something in English he did not understand, set down a tray bearing a pot of coffee and a pot of tea and a note scribbled in Russian: "Breakfast is ready whenever you are." While drinking tea, Belenko noticed laid out on a chair a pair of slacks, a sports shirt, socks, T-shirts, and boxer shorts, but not having been expressly told they were his, he put on his hybrid Japanese suit and went to the dining room.

There Jim introduced him to Peter, one of the three Americans who were to affect his future most significantly. Peter looked the way Belenko thought an artist or composer should; in fact, his countenance, distinguished by a handsome head of dark, curly hair, a delicate face, and black, meditative eyes, reminded Belenko of a portrait of Beethoven he had seen as a boy.

Peter was a devout Catholic, the father of eight children, an accomplished linguist, and one of the best clandestine officers the United States had. Out of the Army and graduate school, he had come to the CIA in 1950, two years after its organization. For a quarter of a century he had fought around the world on some of the fiercest and most pitiless battlefields of the subterranean war that continued to rage without pause between the Soviet Union and the West. Through combat, he had acquired an intuitive feel, an uncommon understanding of Soviet society, culture, history, the language, mentality, and ethnic idiosyncrasies of Russians.

Probably Peter still would have been somewhere abroad had he not contracted on an Asian mission a rare disease for which no cure was known. He was brought home in hope that medical researchers might devise one. Unless they succeeded, he did not have many years to live. Because of disability provisions and tax benefits, he would have profited financially by retiring. He had resolved, however, to fight as long as his body allowed.

Peter amused and relaxed Belenko, bantering with him as if they were meeting for nothing more serious than a game of golf and telling Russian jokes.

"Did you hear about the very sincere Armenian students? They went to a learned professor and asked, 'Is it truly possible to build communism in Armenia?'

"'Yes,' replied the professor, 'but why not do it to the Georgians first?'"

"That's funny; and true, too."

Having changed into the slacks and shirt procured for him before he awoke, Belenko met his "baby-sitter," Nick, who was his age. Born of Russian parents, Nick was a Marine sergeant who had volunteered for two tours in Vietnam and, Belenko surmised, at one time or another had engaged in secret operations against the Russians. He, crewcut, bulging biceps, quick reflexes, unquestioning obedience, and all, was on loan to the CIA. Confident, trained for trouble, Nick could relate to Belenko as a peer and somewhat as a Russian as well as an American. He was to be in the next weeks companion, guide, friend, and, although it was not put that way, bodyguard.

The countryside of northern Virginia, wooded, rolling, and with the foothills of the Blue Ridge Mountains visible from far away on a clear day, is beautiful in all seasons. But it was the man-made order of the farmlands they passed that most struck Belenko: the symmetry of the fields; the perfection of their cultivation; the well-maintained fences; the fatness of the cattle grazing in lush meadows; the painted barns; the white farmhouses that to him seemed huge; the cars, trucks, and machinery parked nearby; the apparent paucity of people working the farms.

"Where are the outhouses?" he asked.

The Americans laughed, and Peter explained how septic tanks and automatic water pumps made possible indoor plumbing in virtually all American farmhouses. "Probably there still are outhouses in some rural or mountainous regions. I just don't know where."

They stopped at a shopping center on the outskirts of a small Virginia town and headed toward a clothing store, but Belenko insisted on inspecting a supermarket on the way. He noticed first the smell or rather the absence of smell; then he explored and stared in ever-widening wonder. Mountains of fruit and fresh vegetables; a long bin of sausages, frankfurters, wursts, salami, bologna, cold cuts; an equally long shelf of cheeses, thirty or forty different varieties; milk, butter, eggs, more than he had ever seen in any one place; the meat counter, at least twenty meters long, with virtually every kind of meat in the world—wrapped so you could take it in your hands, examine, and choose or not; labeled and graded as to quality. A date stamped on the package to warn when it would begin to spoil! And hams and chickens and turkeys! Cans and packages of almost everything edible with pictures showing their contents and labels reciting their contents. Long aisles of frozen foods, again with pictures on the packages. And juices, every kind of juice. Soaps and paper products and toiletries and much else that he did not recognize. Beer! American, German, Dutch, Danish, Australian, Mexican, Canadian beer; all cold. (How many times had he thought and even urged during seminars with the political officers that people be offered low-alcohol beer instead of vodka?) Nobody doled any of this out. You picked it out for yourself and put it in fancy, clear little bags and then in a big, expensive cart. It was all just there for anybody to take.

Turning into an aisle lined on one side with candies, confections, and nuts and on the other with cookies, crackers, and cakes, he saw another "nigger," who cheerfully bade him "Good morning." (There was no gainsaying it; the "nigger" was a handsome fellow except for his color, he did not look like a slave, and he was dressed in the same clean light-blue uniforms the other store workers wore.)

Never had Belenko been in a closed market selling meat or produce that did not smell of spoilage, of unwashed bins and counters, of decaying, unswept remnants of food. Never had he been in a market offering anything desirable that was not crowded inside, with lines waiting outside. Always he had been told that the masses of exploited Americans lived in the shadow of hunger and that pockets of near starvation were widespread, and he had seen photographs that seemed to demonstrate that.

If this were a real store, a woman in less than an hour could buy enough food in just this one place to feed a whole family for two weeks. But where are the people, the crowds, the lines? Ah, that proves it. This is not a real store. The people can't afford it. If they could, everybody would be here. It's a showplace of the Dark Forces. But what do they do with all the meat, fruit and vegeta-

bles, milk, and everything else that they can't keep here all the time? They must take it away for themselves every few nights and replace it.

As Peter and Nick steered him back toward the clothing store, Belenko bolted into a shop offering televisions, stereos, radios, and calculators. Several color television sets were tuned to different channels, and the brilliance and clarity of the hues as well as the diversity of the programs amazed him. So did a hand-held calculator and the technology it implied. But he was not fooled. A color television set in the Soviet Union cost a worker approximately five months' wages, and because of difficulties with transistors and solid-state circuitry, the quality was poor. Obviously this was another showplace of the Dark Forces packed with merchandise affordable only by the exceedingly rich.

He had to appraise the clothing store only a minute or so to realize that it also was a fake. Here were perhaps 300 suits, along with sports jackets, overcoats, raincoats hanging openly on racks, piles of trousers and shirts lying openly on counters, ties within the reach of anybody passing; even the shoes were out in the open—and all this was guarded by only a few clerks. Peter found a section containing perhaps twenty-five suits Belenko's size and started taking them from the rack for him to examine. *They know him here, and that's why he can do that.*

A toothy, glad-handing salesman approached and among other banalities remarked, "It always makes me glad to see a father buying suits for his sons." Belenko thought that whether planned or spontaneous, the comment, which Nick translated in a whisper, was hilarious, and thereafter Peter was known as Father Peter.

The three-piece flannel suit he selected at the advice of Peter required slight alterations, and the salesman suggested they could be made within half an hour if they had other shopping. More evidence. Who else but the Dark Forces could command such service? They purchased shirts, ties, underwear, socks, a warm-up suit and tennis shoes for jogging, a blazer, a raincoat with zip-out lining, and the finest pair of shoes Belenko had ever seen.

All of Belenko's suspicions about the true nature of the shopping center were fully and finally validated when he saw a service station on the corner. Three cars, all, as it happened, driven by women, were being fueled at the same time, a boy was cleaning the windshield of one car, and there were no lines. In Belenko's past life, gasoline outlets were so scarce that a wait of four or five hours for fuel was ordinary.

"I congratulate you," Belenko said en route back to the mansion. "That was a spectacular show you put on for me."

"What do you mean?"

"I mean that place; it's like one of our show *kolkhozes* where we take foreigners."

Nick laughed, but not Peter. "Viktor, I give you my word that what you've just seen is a common, typical shopping center. There are tens of thousands of them all over America. Anywhere you go in the United States, north, south, east, west, you will see pretty much the same. Many of the shopping centers in the suburbs of our cities are bigger and fancier and nicer."

"Can the average American worker buy what we saw there? Can he buy a color television set?"

"Yes; if he's willing to pay more than for a black-and-white set, he can. I don't know what the statistics are; I would guess more families have color sets than not. It's nothing to own a color television. But look, don't take my word. Wait until you travel around and see for yourself."

Why argue with him? That's his job.

The CIA had sent some thirty books and magazines in Russian to his room, and Peter urged him to read, relax, and sleep as much as he could. He showed him a well-stocked liquor cabinet, the kitchen and refrigerator crammed with food, including smoked salmon, herring, and cold borscht, and he pointed out the room where Nick always could be reached. "I almost forgot. Come on."

From another bedroom Peter started pushing a portable

color television set toward Belenko's room, but after a few paces he stopped. "Nick, would you mind?" For the first time Belenko discerned that there was something physically wrong with Peter. If he exerted himself even slightly, he could barely breathe.

That afternoon and evening Belenko experienced another transcendent spiritual upheaval as he read *The Gulag Archipelago*. In the blackness and iniquity of the concentration camps Solzhenitsyn depicts he saw the light and purity of truth, and he trembled again as he had in the Japanese prison. He finished about 10:00 P.M, took a beer from the refrigerator, and, attracted by the brightness of the moonlight and fragrance of the country air, decided to drink it on the veranda. As he opened the door, two men sprang up simultaneously, one with a pistol in hand. "Please excuse us," he said in poor Russian. "We did not know it was you. Come out and make yourself at home."

The Dark Forces, they are not stupid. They would not tell me I could see anywhere what I saw today unless that is true—or unless they intend to imprison me or kill me. But if they're going to kill me or imprison me, what do they care what I think? I don't know. It can't be true. But if it is true, if what I saw is everywhere, then something is very right here.

Jogging around the grounds early in the morning, Belenko saw a little red convertible roar up the driveway at an imprudent speed and screech to a stop. *That's a crazy car. Whoever heard of a car without a top? The driver must be crazy, too. But what a girl!*

Out stepped a voluptuous, lithe young woman, whose beguiling brown eyes and windblown auburn hair made her look wild and mischievous to him. Anna, as she called herself, spoke Russian melodiously and with the fluency of a native, but she was from the Midwest, having mastered the language in school and during travels in the Soviet Union. Her command of the contemporary vernacular, her seemingly encyclopedic knowledge of his homeland, and the skill with which she put him at ease, persuaded Belenko that she worked closely with the important Russians who had taken refuge in the United States.

Because she continuously studied the Soviet Union from perspectives denied him, Anna was able to fascinate and enlighten Belenko with facts and vistas he had not heard or seen before. Her revelations concerning the dissident movement and *samizdat* (underground) publishing in the Soviet Union as well as the number, diversity, and influence of Soviet nationals who had preceded him to the West surprised and heartened him. *I am not alone then. Others have realized, too.*

And her demonstrable understanding of the Soviet Union persuaded him that she might also understand him. She was the first person to whom he could release the accumulated and repressed thoughts, anger, hatred that had driven him away. Once the flow began, it swelled into a torrent, and Anna, who had indicated she would leave at noon, stayed the day to listen.

In listening to Belenko during these first days, the overriding purpose of Peter, Anna and other CIA officers was to assess him as a human being and, accordingly, to propose any modifications in standard resettlement procedures likely to help him adjust and adapt. Luckily for both Belenko and the United States, they did understand him well. And their analysis and recommendations were to permanently and felicitously shape the behavior of the government toward him. Despite the simultaneous clamor from various segments of the intelligence community for an opportunity to question him, the CIA restricted his debriefings to an absolute limit of four hours a day. It allocated his first two working hours, when he would be freshest, to tutoring in English, the one tool most indispensable to his new life. Afternoons and evenings were reserved for reading, study, and excursions planned to show him American life. Save for a few installations, he would be shown anything in the country he asked to see, however inconvenient the showing. And on weekends he would fly, actually take the controls, soar, zoom, dive, roll.

The value of the MiG-25 alone was so immense as to defy

calculation in monetary terms, and the CIA fully intended to guarantee Belenko a secure and affluent future. But pending his final resettlement, there would be no mention of money or compensation unless he broached the subject.

These decisions reflected several basic conclusions about Belenko. He craved freedom and independence, although his concept of freedom was far from crystallized in his mind. Presently, flying symbolized freedom to him, and he had to fly. Otherwise, he would feel himself imprisoned, and the consequent frustrations might erupt in the form of aberrant behavior. While he unavoidably would be dependent during his work with the government and initial orientation to the United States, his social integration must begin at once so he could see that he was progressing toward ultimate independence and self-reliance. His motivation was purely ideological, and he would be affronted unless his contributions were accepted in the same spirit he offered them. Any suggestion that he had fled for materialistic reasons, that he had come to sell the MiG-25 and his information, would cheapen Americans in his eyes and confirm the worst the party said about them. He must be treated as neither merchant nor ward but as a teammate. Finally, he would believe nothing which he could not see, then comprehend through his own thought processes. One should and must tell him the truth, show him the truth. But in the end, he would have to discover the truth for himself.

Belenko was incredulous when Peter and Anna generally outlined the program charted for him without, of course, explaining much of the rationale behind it. The stated willingness of the Americans to let him fly, much less so soon, impressed and touched him. It all sounded so logical, so sensible, so generous, so good. *It is too good to be true. They are just being clever in ways I do not know. They will not let me see everything. I will test them and make them reveal themselves.*

Sure that he was asking the impossible, Belenko said he most wanted to tour a U.S. Air Force fighter base and go aboard an aircraft carrier. Peter acted as if the requests were routine and reasonable. The visit to an air base posed no problem; the Air Force should be able to arrange it within a couple of weeks. As for the carrier, he would have to ascertain from the Navy when one would be close enough ashore for them to fly out. It would just be a question of when. *Father Peter, he's a good actor.*

An emergency or problem of surpassing urgency delayed the beginning of the announced regimen. In the note Belenko drafted in English back in Chuguyevka after he decided to flee, he intended to say, "Contact a representative of the American intelligence service. Conceal and guard the aircraft. Do not allow anyone near it." What he actually wrote in the language he never had studied or heard spoken was: "Quickly call representative American intelligence service. Airplane camouflage. Nobody not allowed to approach." When the Japanese translated the message from English into their own language, the meaning that emerged was: ". . . Aircraft booby-trapped. Do not touch it."

Gingerly peering into the cockpit, the Japanese were further alarmed by the red buttons labeled in Russian "Danger." Apprehensions heightened when they and their American collaborators surmised that the safety catches which would prevent the buttons from doing whatever they were supposed to do were missing. If someone accidentally touched something, would the priceless MiG-25 blow up? Until definitive answers were forthcoming, examination of the plane could not begin, and only Belenko could supply the answers.

So on his third day in America, Air Force officers brought to the mansion huge photographs of the MiG-25 cockpit blown up to its actual size, with resolution so fine that you could see every instrument and inch of the cockpit just as clearly as if you were sitting in it. The leader of the group was a tall, powerfully built colonel with searching dark eyes and the weathered face of a lumberjack. The colonel, introduced as Gregg, shocked Belenko when he spoke. Peter spoke Russian well, Anna spoke it flawlessly, but this colonel spoke Russian as if he had been born and lived all his life in Russia. *He is a*

Russian in disguise! No, that cannot be; that is ridiculous. But what if it is true? Call Nick. Don't make a fool of yourself. You have put your life in their hands anyway. It's their responsibility.

Gregg welcomed Belenko, cordially but not extravagantly, rather as if he were greeting a highly recommended young officer reporting to his squadron. There was important work to do, and he wanted to get on with it. They set up the panels of photographs in the library, creating an eerily accurate three-dimensional illusion of the cockpit, and placed against the wall photographs displaying various sections, actual size.

Belenko explained what he understood to be the purpose of each button marked "Danger." He could not explain why the safety pins had been removed; they were supposed to be there. A drunken mistake? Malice by someone in the regiment? Orders? He honestly did not know. But together, he and Gregg figured out where to insert replacement pins, which Japanese and American technicians would have to fabricate.

"Okay, now show me how to start the engines."

"Why not wait until we have it over here? I can show you everything then and teach your pilots how to fly it."

"I'm afraid we're not going to be able to fly it. It looks as if we'll have to give it back in a month or so."

"What! Are you stupid?" Belenko was incredulous, enraged, betrayed. "Give it back! Do you think that if an F-14 or F-15 landed in Czechoslovakia or Poland, you would ever get it back? It's *your* airplane now! I brought it to you! I risked my life, I gave up everything to give it to you! Make the Japanese let you have it! If you give it back, the Russians will laugh at you! They will think you are fools!"

"Calm down!" Gregg commanded. "I'm as pissed off as you are. I agree with you. But I don't make policy. We figure with your help we can learn most of what we need to know without flying it. So let's get started."

It's unbelievable. What can I do? I guess nothing except help them as much as I can.

As they worked together, two professionals addressing a common task, Belenko increasingly realized he was talking with an authentic flier and a man who spoke his language in every way. The more he learned of the colonel, the surer he was of his initial impression. For Gregg was everything that Belenko had aspired to be—fighter pilot, combat pilot, test pilot, adventurer. In Vietnam he had flown 100 Wild Weasel missions over Hanoi, Haiphong, and the nests of SAMs protecting strategic bridges, and from his lessons in American tactics, Belenko knew what these missions were. Wild Weasel pilots, usually flying F-105s, were the first to venture into a target area and the last to leave. They flew about trying to provoke the SAM crews into turning on the radar that guided the missiles and firing at them. Quite simply, they dangled their lives before the North Vietnamese and their Soviet advisers. If the SAM crews rose to the bait, other American aircraft could lock onto the ground radar and fire; Shrike missiles would follow the radar beam down to its source, obliterating the SAM site, crews and all. If the Wild Weasel pilots were lucky, they would see or their instruments would detect the arrays of SAMs rocketing toward them at three times the speed of sound. Then they could flout death by diving at sharp angles a SAM could not emulate. If they did not see the SAM, which looked like a flying telephone pole, if they did not dive quickly enough, if they were caught in the inferno of ground fire that erupted as they pulled out of the dive to go back up as live decoys, they would not know what happened. A sympathetic telegram from the Defense Department, however, would inform their wives and children back in the States.

Professors at Armavir explained that the Wild Weasel pilots were willing to offer up their lives because (1) they were highly paid mercenaries or (2) they were under the influence of marijuana or stronger narcotics. Belenko believed neither explanation and had asked himself, *Would I be so brave? Could I do that?*

Gregg's parents, like Nick's, were Russian émigrés, and

determined to impart some of their native culture to their children, they insisted on speaking Russian in the home, and he studied the language throughout his university years. Because of his command of the language, as well as the technical background acquired as a test pilot, Gregg frequently had been diverted, against his will, from flying to intelligence assignments. He had gained the respect and confidence of the CIA, not given lightly to outsiders, and hence, it was decided that he should be primarily responsible for the technical debriefing of Belenko. As it developed, there could have been no better choice.

The personal rapport that evolved between Belenko and his three principal American stewards failed, however, to demolish the barricade of skepticism which guarded him against the wiles of the Dark Forces. He did not blame Peter, Anna, and Gregg or the Dark Forces for presenting him with the most roseate picture of their country. That was their duty; he understood. He merely remained disposed to disbelieve much of what they said and to regard what he saw as atypical.

Certainly, nothing could convince him that the garden apartment in Falls Church, Virginia, where he and Nick settled was approximately typical of those being constructed in the Washington suburbs and within the means of young couples with a moderate income. *Whoever heard of a worker's apartment with two bathrooms and carpets all over the floors and machines that wash the dishes and do away with the garbage? And a special room for reading [a small den]. Of course not.*

True to their word, the Dark Forces arranged for him to fly from Andrews Air Force Base outside Washington to visit a fighter base. He and Gregg were waiting in the departure lounge when the wing commander at Andrews, a general, strode in, recognized Gregg, and came over to shake hands. Belenko was incredulous because the general was black. *He's not a real nigger. No nigger could be a general. They must have painted somebody and dressed him in a general's uniform. Sure, they painted him just for me.*

The fighter base, he judged, artfully combined the authentically representative with the seductively phony embroidered to impress selected visitors like him. He was invited to inspect the fighters, F-4s, F-106s, and then one of the two he had been taught most to dread, the F-15. "Go ahead, sit in the cockpit," Gregg said. "But if you fly away with one of these, they'll have my ass." No question; the fighters were real enough, just as they had been described in the Soviet Union. Some attributes did surprise him. The electronic, fire control, armament, navigational, and certain other systems were much more sophisticated than he had been told, and the exterior surfaces of all the U.S. planes were smoother than those of the MiG-25. Essentially, though, they were what he expected: marvelous machines, but known machines.

The clubs for enlisted personnel, noncommissioned officers, and officers, with their various rooms for dining, dancing, drinking, reading, pool, Ping-Pong, cards, and chess; the athletic fields, gymnasiums, swimming pools, tennis courts; the theater—they *might* be real.

"How can you afford to spend so much on people rather than weapons?"

"How can we afford not to?" responded the fighter-base commander, a colonel, who was escorting them. "The best weapons in the world are no good unless you have people willing and able to man them."

That's right, absolutely right. That's what I was trying to tell the Party.

The base commander told Belenko that the Air Force wished to give him an American flight suit as a memento of the visit. Never had he admired any apparel so much. Although made of synthetics, it was silken and flexible in feel, light, yet warm. "You make a fine-looking American pilot," Gregg said, as Belenko looked at himself in the dark green suit before a mirror.

"Let me show you something," said an officer, who flicked a cigarette lighter and touched the flame to the flight suit.

"Don't do that!" shouted Belenko, shoving the officer away.

"No, just trust me. It's fireproof. If it burns, we'll give you a new one." The officer held the flame to a sleeve, and Belenko saw that the suit was, indeed, impervious to fire.

Belenko then asked to meet a typical sergeant, whom he questioned about his work and standard of living. Believing none of the straightforward answers, Belenko announced he would like to visit the sergeant's quarters. Easy enough, said the commander. He lives only a few blocks away. Come on, we'll go in my car. Obviously, this was a put-on. *Can you imagine a colonel actually driving people around, including one of his own sergeants, like a common chauffeur?*

The sergeant lived on base in a two-story stucco house with a screened front porch, small yard, and attached garage. Belenko asked how a sergeant could have such a large house, and the commander told him the size of the house allotted depended on the size of the family to occupy it. *Oh, that's absurd. And look at that car [a 1976 Impala]! They want me to think a sergeant owns a car like that. Why, it's better than the colonel's car.*

Upon looking at a major's house, which was nicer but not that much nicer, Belenko gave up. *I've seen the show. Why put them to more trouble?*

That evening some officers took Belenko and Gregg to a good dinner at a civilian restaurant near the base. Belenko felt that the conversation, pilots talking to pilots, was genuine and stimulating. But when the host attempted to pay the check, the whole scheme was exposed to him. The proprietor, a Greek immigrant, refused to take money, and the meal cost well over $100. Gregg translated. "He says he owes this country more than he can ever repay, but as a token repayment he is giving us dinner. I think he's guessed or someone has told him who you are."

Sometimes, though, Belenko saw significance in the mundane, and some of his observations began to engender doubts about his doubts. On successive Sundays, Peter took him to the zoo in Washington's Rock Creek Park and the King's Dominion Amusement Park north of Richmond. The zoo, situated in lovely woods, maintains a large collection of exotic animals. The amusement park is a wholesome place offering many ingenious rides and delights for children and teenagers. Yet at both the zoo and park he was most impressed by the people.

Most, in his opinion, were from the "working class." Try as he would, he could not honestly discern in their appearance or behavior any manifestations of the fear, anxiety, or privation which he from childhood on had been assured prevailed among the majority of Americans. Families and couples strolled about as if, for the moment anyway, they were carefree and having a good time. Among them were many black people. They were dressed just as well as the white people, were equally attentive to their children, and, so far as he could tell, seemed to have no qualms about mingling with the white people.

He momentarily froze, then pointed at a rather pretty young blond girl holding hands with a young black man at the amusement park. "Is that allowed in this country?"

"It's their business," Peter said. "Not ours, not the government's."

There was something else. According to the Party, zoos, museums, and other public recreational facilities in the United States cost so much that ordinary people could not afford them. But as he verified for himself, admission to the zoo was free, and while the rides at the park cost money, the workers, including the blacks, obviously could afford them.

He doubted that the zoo and park were Potemkin creations of the Dark Forces, as he had thought the shopping center, mansion, apartment, and air base were. His Sunday observations did not convince him that the United States was a land of universal contentment, justice, and racial equality.

But if what he saw was fairly representative, then social and economic conditions were vastly different from what the Party said. *If this is true, they're bigger liars than I ever dreamed. If this is true, then something is right here.*

It took Peter and Nick a while to locate "a real workers' bar, a cheap place," where the lowly laborers might repair in the evening, but they found an approximation on a side street in Falls Church. There was a long bar with stools on one side and a row of wooden booths on the other. Men in working clothes were drinking beer, talking, and laughing or watching a savage game (Monday night football) on color television. The menu of the establishment was chalked on a blackboard, and although Belenko already had dined, he insisted on sampling the food, which he ordered at random. A black man served an extravagant portion of barbecued beef sandwiched in a large bun, together with french fried potatoes, coleslaw, and a beer. The little green check totaled $2.08.

That was real meat, delicious, and so cheap. And I think that black man made it himself and was proud of it. The men's room was clean. Nobody was drunk or vomiting or fighting. Come to think of it, I haven't seen drunks or fighting on the streets here. But there are bars everywhere here. You can buy vodka and beer and wine here a lot easier than in the Soviet Union. And it's so cheap, people could stay drunk all the time if they wanted. It's as if 1980 has already come!

When Belenko expressed some of these thoughts, Peter remarked, "I'm sorry to say that alcoholism is a serious problem in the United States. By our definition, between nine and ten million Americans are alcoholics."

"What is your definition of an alcoholic?"

"Someone who is dependent on alcohol or whose consumption of alcohol harmfully interferes with his or her life."

"Well, by that definition, three-fourths of all the men in the Soviet Union are alcoholics."

Peter agreed that alcoholism was a more acute problem in the Soviet Union than in the United States but went on to explain the American problem with drug addiction.

Referring to purveyors of illicit drugs, Belenko exclaimed, "Why don't you arrest them? Shoot them! Or at least put them in jail!"

"We try to arrest them. But, Viktor, as you will learn, it is not so easy to put someone in jail in the United States."

Both Peter and Anna emphasized to Belenko the necessity of learning to drive, a task he relished. Upon being told that prior to his lessons he would have to obtain a Virginia learner's permit, he was incensed.

"Why can't you just give me a license?"

"We don't have the power to do that."

"That is ridiculous. In the Soviet Union you can buy a license on the black market for a hundred rubles. If you can't issue me a license, buy me one."

"Take my word, Viktor, you're going to have to pass a test like everybody else. We can give you false identity papers, but not a license."

Belenko learned to drive in less than an hour but tended to maneuver a car as if it were a fighter plane and habitually exceeded the speed limit. He was driving with Peter along a four-lane divided highway, when a siren sounded behind them.

"God dammit, Viktor, you're speeding. Now do as I tell you. Slow down, pull off the highway, and stop and roll down the window. The state trooper will come up and ask for your driver's license. Just give it to him, and say nothing. He will write a ticket. When he hands it to you, just nod and say, 'Thank you, Officer.'"

Belenko was unconcerned; indeed, he welcomed the opportunity to demonstrate to Peter his ability to cope with the unexpected. He knew what to do. Every 100 kilometers or so along Soviet roads, police maintain checkpoints and routinely stop all vehicles. The driver routinely gives the policeman two or three rubles; otherwise, he is accused and convicted on the spot of a traffic violation, and his license is punched and, with the third punch, revoked.

A tall state trooper wearing a broad-brimmed gray hat

bent down by the window. "Son, do you realize you were going eighty-five miles an hour?"

Belenko grinned and tried to hand the trooper two twenty-dollar bills.

"No! No!" Peter yelled in Russian. "Take that money back, Viktor!" Then in English: "Officer, I am a representative of the Central Intelligence Agency. May I speak with you privately?" Peter got out of the car and talked with the trooper.

After a couple of minutes the trooper returned and said to Belenko, "I would like to shake your hand."

With a seriousness that Belenko did not mistake, Peter warned that bribery of a policeman or public official was a major crime. "Some will take bribes, that's true. But ninety-nine point nine percent won't, and if you try it, you will be arrested, and I may not always be around to rescue you. I'm telling you for your own good."

Father Peter, he means what he says. But if officials don't take bribes, maybe the law is the same for everybody. Well, that's right, they put Nixon's men in jail.

The Party depicted America as awash in pornography, a social pox communism spares the Soviet Union. Having seen none in the Virginia suburbs, Belenko asked where all the pornography was, so Peter took him to an X-rated movie. "What did you think?" he asked as they left the theater a few blocks from the White House.

"At first I was amazed. Then I felt as if I were watching people go to the toilet. Nobody loved anybody in that movie. What I don't understand is why, if pornography is so popular, the theater was so empty."

"Obviously, there's a market for the stuff, or the theater couldn't stay in business. But which would you rather do? Watch some whores go through the motions of making love or go out and find a girl and make love yourself?"

Anna invited Belenko to a Washington restaurant to meet her husband, an urbane, older man who was highly informed about the Soviet Union and spoke Russian confidently. Because Belenko was conditioned to believe that American presidential elections were meaningless, all candidates being puppets of the Dark Forces, he listened with surprise and interest as his host talked about the contest under way between Gerald Ford and Jimmy Carter. Anna favored Carter; her husband, Ford. They discussed, then debated, then ardently and angrily argued about the qualifications of the two candidates.

Wait a minute. Maybe elections here do make a difference. At least they think they do, and they are not fools.

It was the carrier, or rather, what he deduced from the carrier, that finally shattered the image of America instilled by the Party. He and Gregg landed on its deck in a small plane about 100 miles off the Virginia capes. The captain welcomed Belenko by saying that the United States Navy was proud to have him as its guest. He could see anything aboard the ship he desired; any question would be answered. But the captain believed that first he should watch the launching and recovery of aircraft, the essence of carrier operations.

As Belenko stood by the landing control officer, the fighters plummeted, thundered, roared down straight toward him. Bam! Screech! They hit the steel deck and crashed into the arresting gear. Then, with a tremendous roar that vibrated his body, the afterburners of a fighter ignited, and it shot off the deck, dipped toward the sea, and rocketed out of sight. This, every ten seconds!

_ No show could have been more spectacular to Belenko. The technology of the ship, the planes, the diverse individual skills of the crew were incredible. But that was not what was most meaningful. Everybody of all ranks participating in the operation relied, depended on, indeed, trusted their lives to everybody else. Nobody abused anybody. They all were one team, and it couldn't be any other way. You couldn't terrify, intimidate, threaten, or coerce men into doing what they were doing. They had to want to do it, to believe in it. They couldn't do it under the influence of drugs or alcohol. And this was real. The Dark Forces did not construct this carrier or recruit and train these men just to put on a display for him.

Now he was inclined to believe what he saw and was told.

"Do you have a jail on this ship?"

They showed him the brig—five or six immaculate cells with standard Navy bunks—which happened to be empty.* In answer to his questions, the captain enumerated some of the offenses for which a sailor might be confined—drinking alcohol, smoking marijuana, assault.

"Why is your jail empty?"

"Maybe we're lucky. We don't have much trouble aboard this ship."

"How many people do you have on this ship?"

"About five thousand officers and men."

It's a small city, and nobody is in jail!

Noticing the insignia of the cross on the shirt collar of an officer, Belenko asked if the crew was required to profess faith in God.

The captain replied that although Protestant, Catholic, and Jewish chaplains regularly conducted services, crew members were free to attend or not and that religious beliefs or the lack of them was entirely a private matter of individual conscience.

Belenko wanted to know if the chaplains additionally functioned as political officers, and the captain did not at first understand what he meant.

"Who tells your men how they must vote?" He realized that the laughter the question caused was real and spontaneous. *If nobody can even tell the soldiers* [enlisted men] *how to vote, then they do have some freedom here.*

The carrier was the flagship of an admiral who presented Belenko with a fleece-lined leather jacket worn by Navy pilots. He said he hoped Belenko would wear and regard it as a symbol of the appreciation and comradeship U.S. Navy fliers felt toward him. The gift and words so affected him that

* Had it been occupied, Belenko would probably not have been allowed to see it.

he spoke with difficulty. "I will be very proud of this jacket."

He was so proud of the jacket that throughout the day he carried it with him wherever he went. All life had taught him that left unguarded, such valuable apparel certainly would be stolen.

"Viktor, leave that damn jacket here," Gregg said as they started from the cabin to see the evening movie.

"No, someone will steal it."

"Nobody will steal it. This is not a pirate ship."

"No, I know somebody will steal it."

After much argument, against all good judgment and under vehement protest, Belenko reluctantly obeyed and left the jacket on his bunk. During the movie he fidgeted and worried. "I think I'll go back and see about my jacket."

"Sit still. Your jacket is all right." Later Gregg slipped away to the cabin and hid the jacket in a closet.

Returning from the movie, Belenko saw that the worst had happened. "You see! I told you! I told you! They stole it!" Gregg opened the closet, and Belenko grabbed the jacket, clutched it, hugged it, and did not let it out of his sight again.

The excellence, abundance, and variety of food in the enlisted men's mess did not bespeak exploitation of a lower class or reflect a national scarcity of food. The provision of such food—and nowhere except aboard the 747 had he tasted better—was consistent with the Air Force officer's remark at the Air Force base about the importance of caring for people.

The admiral in his cabin opened a refrigerator and apologized that he could offer only a soft drink or fruit juice. Surely an admiral can have a drink in his own quarters if he wants? "No, I'm afraid we all have to abide by the rules." The reply was consistent with what Father Peter had told him about the law.

Everything I've seen is consistent. Every time I have been able to check what the Party said it has turned out to be a lie. Every time I have been able to check what Father Peter and Anna and Gregg say it has turned out to be true. Something is very right in this country. I don't understand what it is, how it works. But I think the Americans are much farther along toward building True Communism than the Soviet Union ever will be.

A couple of days after they flew back from the carrier, Peter recounted to Belenko all the Soviet Union had been saying about him and all it was doing to recapture him. "They realize that we will not give you up and that their only chance is to persuade you to return voluntarily. So, almost daily, they demand from us another opportunity to talk to you. They're being rather clever, if brutal, about it. They know they can't do anything to us directly. Therefore, they are trying to pressure us indirectly through the Japanese. They're seizing Japanese fishing boats, threatening and harassing the Japanese in every way they can. And I'm afraid they won't stop until we let them see you once more."

"What do they say?"

"Oh, it's all bullshit. They say they're not sure the man they saw in Tokyo was you and that, in any case, they did not have long enough to determine whether you were acting voluntarily or under duress."

"What do you want me to do?"

"Only you can decide. You do not have to meet them. But the Japanese have been valiant and steadfast throughout, and it would be a big service to them if you would."

"All right. Let's get it over. But I tell you, and you can tell them, this is the last time."

Peter and several other CIA officers, including a couple of unfamiliar, tough-looking characters who comported with his original concept of CIA men, led Belenko to the anteroom of a conference hall at the State Department. "We will be waiting right here and will come immediately if there is trouble. We have made sure that they are in no way armed. You will be safe. Just be yourself."

Waiting in the conference chamber were Minister-Counselor Vorontsov, the chief Soviet representative at the Belgrade conference on human rights, a Soviet physician, and a KGB officer, who posed as a diplomat at the Soviet Embassy in Washington.

As soon as Belenko entered, Vorontsov warmly clasped his hand. "It always is good to meet a man from our Mother Country." Immediately trying to establish psychological control, he said, as if he, rather than the State Department, were in charge of the meeting, "Please sit down, and let's talk freely and openly. Now, we know that something happened to your aircraft and that you did not land in Japan voluntarily.

"We know that in Japan you tried to protect your aircraft by firing your pistol," Vorontsov continued. "We know that the Japanese employed force against you and clamped a bag on your head. We know that the Japanese put you in prison and drugged you with narcotics. We know that your actions and movements have not been voluntary.

"Your wife and son, all your relatives are grieving, crying, longing for you. Here, they have sent letters and photographs for you." Vorontsov laid them on the table before Belenko, who ignored them. Vorontsov pushed them closer. Belenko looked away from them and glowered directly into Vorontsov's eyes, provoking, he thought, a flicker of anger. But Vorontsov, a forceful man, retained his composure and went on, calmly, seductively.

"We want you to know that despite all that has happened and even if you did make some mistake, you will be forgiven completely if you return to your Mother Country, to your family, your native land, the only land where you ever can be happy. You need not be afraid. I reiterate and promise on the highest possible authority that you will be forgiven.

"Let me give you an example. A Soviet major defected to the United States and, after meeting with us, chose to return to our Mother Country. Later he went to the American Embassy in Moscow and assured the Americans that he was free and not being punished."

At this an American, a cool young State Department official whom Belenko had not previously noticed, burst into laughter. "That is not true, Mr. Vorontsov."

"That's the trouble with you Americans," Vorontsov shouted. "You never believe us."

"Not when you lie like that."

Returning to Belenko, Vorontsov said, "My comrade, if you wish, you may leave this room with us right now, and tomorrow you will be in Moscow reunited with your family in your Mother Country. And you can continue your career as a pilot." Here Vorontsov beamed. "In fact, I am authorized to assure you that you can become a test pilot."

Belenko stood up. "Let me speak clearly and finally. All I did, before and after I landed in Japan, I did voluntarily. The Japanese were kind to me and helped me very much, although it was very difficult for them to do that. They gave me no drugs of any sort. They did not put a bag on my head. They used no force against me. They protected me. Everything I have done, I have done of my own free will. In the United States nobody is keeping me by force or against my will. It is my own wish to be in the United States. I will not return."

Belenko turned to the presiding State Department official. "Although I understand there is a rule that only one Soviet representative may speak to me, I would like to waive that rule and invite the doctor here to ask me any questions he wants because I am absolutely healthy."

That was obvious to the doctor, who seemed somewhat embarrassed, but he had to go through the motions.

"Do you have a headache?"

"No."

"Have you been taking any medicine?"

"No."

"How do you feel?"

"Great."

The doctor looked for guidance from Vorontsov, who now began speaking heatedly. "Our foreign minister is discussing you with Secretary Kissinger and at the highest levels of the American government because we know they are using force and keeping you against your will."

"No, they are not using force or keeping me against my will. I will not return to the Soviet Union."

"What did happen, then? Why did you do this?"

"You can investigate and find out for yourself why."

Vorontsov resumed his unctuous manner. "You will decide to return. When you decide, just call the Soviet Embassy, and you will be welcome back." The KGB officer laid his card on the table.

"I have made my decision. I will not return. I will stay in the United States. There is nothing more to discuss."

The State Department official rose. "All right, gentlemen. It seems to me that our meeting is concluded."

As Belenko walked out, Vorontsov called to him, and there was in his tone a confidence, a sureness that slightly disquieted Belenko. "We know that you will return. We will get you back. You will come someday."

The CIA officers waiting outside each solemnly shook hands with Belenko. "I know that was very hard for you," Peter said. "You are a good and brave man, Viktor."

They drove across Memorial Bridge and into Arlington National Cemetery, then slowly wended their way along narrow lanes among the graves. "What are we doing in the graveyard?" asked Belenko.

"We are making sure that the KGB cannot follow us."

"What! You mean you have those bastards in this country, too!"

"Yes, and it is prudent always to bear that in mind. You will have to bear it in mind for the rest of your life."

From the cemetery, shrouded in beauteous autumn leaves, they commanded a grand view of Washington, which in the late afternoon sunshine looked resplendent. Belenko thought of his new life and a little of his old.

Could they ever get me back? Would I ever go back? No, of course not.

CHAPTER
VII

Unwrapping the Present

For a decade the mystery of the MiG-25 had kindled the gravest of debates, doubts, and apprehensions in the West. The existence of the plane, what was known and unknown about it, had affected defense budgets, aircraft design and production, strategic thinking, and high political decisions of the United States.

On the basis of the best Western evaluations of Soviet technology, the United States did not understand how the Russians in the 1960s could produce a fighter capable of flying at Mach 3.2 and carrying four heavy missiles to an altitude of 80,000 feet—something not even the newest U.S. fighters introduced in the 1970s could do.

Were the fundamental estimates of the level of Soviet technology wrong? Had the Russians secretly achieved momentous breakthroughs in metallurgy, engine, and airframe design, perhaps even avionics, that endowed them with a capacity to attain air superiority over the West? Was the MiG-25 already the best interceptor in the world, as Secretary Seamans said and doubtless believed? Did it already give the Russians a measure of air superiority? If the answers to such questions were affirmative, then the West was in trouble from which it could extricate itself only through costly and urgent efforts, that large segments of the public, disgusted by Vietnam and enamored with détente, might not support. If the answers were negative or largely so, then the United States could allocate resources more efficiently and intelligently to counter real rather than nonexistent threats. So one of the greatest gifts Belenko brought was the opportunity to answer definitively these long-standing questions.

To safeguard Belenko and talk to him securely, the CIA established what appeared to be a medical laboratory in a large office building. People could enter and leave the building without arousing curiosity, no one from the general public was likely to wander into the "laboratory," and anyone approaching could be observed while walking down a long corridor that led to the one entrance. There was, however, a second, hidden exit. And in keeping with the practice of compartmentation, very few people in the CIA itself would know where he was working.

Belenko rose early and made breakfast in time to receive his English tutor, Betsy, who came daily to the apartment at seven. To him, she was a happy sight—stylishly dressed, slender, bright, and eager to teach. They were the same age, liked each other, and worked hard.

After traveling different routes from day to day and periodically checking against surveillance, Belenko and his escort, sometimes Nick, sometimes Gregg, arrived at the office to begin interrogation and debriefings around nine-thirty. No matter how lacking is the evidence to support the conjecture, there always are those willing to speculate that any Soviet defector is actually a controlled Soviet agent dispatched to confuse and confound by purveying false or deceptive information. In any case, prudence dictates that counterintelligence specialists satisfy themselves as to the authenticity and veracity of the defector. One means of so doing is to ask a variety of questions, innocuous, sensitive, arcane, to which the answers are already known, and the initial interrogations of Belenko were heavily laced with such test queries.

"By the way, how do the Russians remove snow from the runways?"

"We use a kind of blower made from a discarded jet engine. If it doesn't succeed or if there is ice, the whole regiment turns out with shovels and picks."

That was correct. So were all of Belenko's other answers, and they corroborated the conclusions of Anna and Peter. Not only was Belenko keenly intelligent, highly knowledgeable, and ideologically motivated, but he was telling the truth. And once the CIA certified him in its own judgment as bona fide, the excitement of unraveling the mystery of the dreaded MiG-25 began in earnest, in America and Japan.

The Americans needed to ascertain first what the MiG-25 Belenko delivered represented. Was it an obsolescent aircraft whose production had been discontinued? Were more advanced models than he flew extant? Was the MiG-25 being superseded by a newer, higher-performance aircraft?

The Russians first flew a MiG-25 prototype in 1964 and began assembly-line production in the late 1960s. After the commanding general of the Soviet Air Defense Command was killed in a MiG-25 crash in 1969, they halted production for about a year but resumed it in 1970 or 1971. Periodically they modified the aircraft, eliminated flaws, and upgraded capabilities. Far from considering the plane obsolete or relegating it to a reconnaissance role, the Russians in 1976 regarded the MiG-25 as their best high-altitude interceptor. And MiG-25s along with MiG-23s were replacing all other aircraft assigned to the Air Defense Command (MiG-17s, MiG-19s, SU-9s, SU-15s, and YAK-28s).

The MiG-25 Belenko landed in Hakodate had rolled out of the factory in February 1976, and the date of manufacture could be deciphered from the serial number stamped on the fuselage. The plane thus was one of the latest models and embodied the highest technology then in production. It was the plane on which the Russians intended to rely as a mainstay of their air defenses for years to come.

Meanwhile, dozens of American aeronautical, electronic,

and metallurgical experts from the United States and else-where joined the Japanese in scientific exploration of the plane itself. The initial, critical task was to ferret out the explosive charges planted to destroy sensitive parts of the plane the Russians were determined no foreigner should ever see—the radar, fire control system, electronic coun-termeasures, computer, automatic pilot. With difficulty, the Americans located and removed the explosives—"something of a cross between a cherry bomb and a stick of dynamite." Then the Japanese and Americans painstakingly removed the wings, horizontal tail fins, afterburners, and pylons and loaded them, together with the fuselage, into a giant U.S. Air Force Galaxy C-5A cargo plane. Some of the Japanese techni-cians lettered and strung on the fuselage a large banner say-ing, "Sayonara, people of Hakodate. Sorry for the trouble."

Soviet fighters still prowled the skies around Hakodate, and fearful that they might interfere, the Japanese cloaked the C-5A within a formation of missile-firing F-104s and F-4s while it transported the MiG to Hyakuri Air Base sixty miles north of Tokyo on September 25. There, in a large hangar guarded by Japanese soldiers, the real unwrapping of the "present for the Dark Forces" began. Some of the Americans had devoted much of their careers to dissecting captured or stolen Soviet equipment, and they, along with their Japanese colleagues, approached the hangar much in the spirit of eager archaeologists allowed temporary entry into a forbidden tomb full of rare and glittering riches which might be sur-veyed but not kept. They had to analyze swiftly and urgently, yet carefully and thoroughly, so the labor was divided among teams which focused day and night upon separate sections or components.

As the entire MiG was disassembled and the engines, radar, computer, automatic pilot, fire control, electronic countermeasure, hydraulic, communications, and other sys-tems were put on blocks and stands for mechanical, elec-tronic, metallurgical, and photographic analysis, the specialists experienced a succession of surprises and shocks.

My God! Look what this thing is made of! Why, the dumb bastards don't have transistors; they're still using vacuum tubes! These engines are monsters! Maybe the Sovs have a separate refinery for each plane! Jesus! See these rivet heads sticking out, and look at that welding! They did it by hand! Hell, the pilot can't see a thing unless it's practically in front of him! This contraption isn't an airplane; it's a rocket! Hey, see what they've done here! How clever! They were able to use aluminum! Why didn't we ever think of that? How ingenious! It's brilliant!

The data Belenko supplied in response to the first quick queries also seemed surprising and, at first, contradictory.

What is the maximum speed of the MiG-25?

You cannot safely exceed Mach 2.8, but actually we were forbidden to exceed Mach 2.5. You see, at high speeds the engines have a very strong tendency to accelerate out of control, and if they go above Mach 2.8, they will overheat and burn up.

But we have tracked the MiG-25 at Mach 3.2.

Yes, and every time it has flown that fast the engines have been completely ruined and had to be replaced and the pilot was lucky to land in one piece. (That fitted with intelligence the Americans had. They knew that the MiG-25 clocked over Israel at Mach 3.2 in 1973 had landed back in Egypt with its engines totally wrecked. They did not understand that the wreckage was inevitable rather than a freakish occurrence.)

What is your combat radius?

At best, 300 kilometers [186 miles].

You're joking!

I am not. If you use afterburners and maneuver for intercept, you can stay up between twenty-two and twenty-seven minutes at the most. Make one pass, and that's it.

We thought the range was 2,000 kilometers [1,240 miles].

Belenko laughed. That's ridiculous. Theoretically, if you don't use afterburners, don't maneuver, and stay at the best altitude, you can fly 1,200 kilometers [744 miles] in a straight line. But in practice, when we were ferrying the plane from base to base, we never tried to fly more than 900 kilometers [558 miles] without refueling. Check it out for yourself. I took off from Chuguyevka with full tanks and barely made it to Japan. You can calculate roughly how far I flew and how much fuel was left when I landed. (The point was convincing. Although Belenko expended fuel excessively during the minutes while at sea level, he used afterburners only briefly and otherwise did everything possible to conserve. Even so, of the 14 tons of fuel with which he began, his flight of less than 500 miles consumed all but 52.5 gallons.)

What is your maximum operational altitude?

That depends. If you carry only two missiles, you can reach 24,000 meters [78,740 feet] for a minute or two. With four missiles, 21,000 meters [68,900] is the maximum.

What is the maximum altitude of your missiles?

They will not work above 27,000 meters [88,580 feet].

Then you cannot intercept the SR-71 [the most modern U.S. reconnaissance plane]!

True; for all sorts of reasons. First of all, the SR-71 flies too high and too fast. The MiG-25 cannot reach it or catch it. Secondly, as I told you, the missiles are useless above 27,000 meters, and as you know, the SR-71 cruises much higher. But even if we could reach it, our missiles lack the velocity to overtake the SR-71 if they are fired in a tail chase. And if they are fired head-on, their guidance systems cannot adjust quickly enough to the high closing speed.

What about your radar?

It's a very good radar. Jamproof. But it cannot distinguish targets below 500 meters [1,640 feet] because of ground clutter.

A MiG-25 cannot intercept a target approaching below 500 meters then?

It cannot.

Maneuvering. Tell us about maneuvering. How many Gs can you take in a turn?

If the tanks are full, there is so much weight in the wings

that they will rip off if you try more than 2.2 Gs. Even if you're almost out of fuel, anything above 5 Gs is dangerous.

The Americans were stunned. Why, you can't turn inside even an F-4!

You can't turn inside anything. It's not designed to dogfight.

Partially because the leaks to the press emanated from sources that had concentrated on individual facets of the aircraft rather than on the plane as a whole, published reports about what was being discovered in Japan were confusing and also contradictory.

A Japanese investigator was quoted: "The comparison of the fire control system of the F-4EJ and the MiG-25 is like that of a miniaturized, modern, precision audio kit and a large old-fashioned electric Gramophone."

Newsweek reported:

> The Japanese experts who gave the plane a preliminary once-over were astonished to find the body and wings covered with spots of brownish rust. Clearly, the MiG wasn't made of the strong lightweight titanium used in U.S. interceptors. But what was it made of? The Japanese pulled out a magnet, and a loud "thunk" confirmed their suspicions: The Foxbat was plated with old-fashioned steel.
>
> That was just the beginning. . . . The welding and riveting were sloppy. It appeared that the plane would be difficult to control in a tight turn, and that at top speed its missiles could be torn from the wings.

Representative Robert Carr wrote a lengthy article suggesting that the Pentagon had deceived the American people by purposely and grossly exaggerating the might of the MiG-25:

> In fact, as a fighter, the Foxbat is barely equal to our 15-year-old McDonnell F-4 Phantom and it is hopelessly outclassed by our new generation McDonnell F-15 and

General Dynamics F-16. Either of our two newer Air Force fighters can outclimb, out-accelerate, out-turn, out-see, out-hide and out-shoot the Foxbat by margins so wide that our expected kill-ratio advantage is almost incalculable. No U.S. F-15 or F-16 pilot need fear the Foxbat unless he is asleep, radically out-numbered or an utter boob.

Yet some American experts examining the MiG-25 were described as awed by what they saw. One said aspects of the plane were "brilliantly engineered." Another commented, "We thought it was a damned good plane, and that's what it turned out to be. We're belittling it because it's unsophisticated or because it rusts. In fact, it can fly higher, faster, and with a bigger payload than any plane in the world." Another: "The MiG-25 does the job well, at less than it would cost the U.S. to build an equivalent plane." And another: "It is apparent that Soviet designers are efficient cost managers who use only as much quality as is needed to solve a problem. They seem to ask why go to the expense of developing something new when we have something proven and cheaper on the shelf. They could come over here and teach us something in the way of cost-conscious management and design."

What was the truth? Were all the furor and alarm over the years wholly unjustified? Was the MiG-25 a "clinker," a "turkey," a flying "Potemkin village"? Had the Pentagon, together with its allies in the aviation industry, conjured up a phony threat to extract money from Congress, as Representative Carr implied? Did not the gift from Belenko reassuringly prove anew the superiority of the West? If so, how had the Russians nonetheless produced an aircraft whose recorded performance exceeded in several ways that of our very best?

The data collected in Japan, then analyzed by the Foreign Technology Division of the Air Force at Dayton, Ohio, and the reports of the ongoing interrogation of Belenko all were flowing into the office of Major General George J. Keegan, Jr., then chief of Air Force Intelligence. As the information was collated to form a single mosaic, clear and definitive answers emerged.

They showed that the West had been badly mistaken in its perceptions of the capability, purpose, menace, and implications of the MiG-25. The misconceptions occurred because the West evaluated the MiG in Western terms and thereby adopted false premises, which only the arrival of Belenko corrected.

Because the MiG-25 had been clocked and tracked flying at Mach 3.2 at 80,000 feet, the West assumed that the recordings reflected the plane's actual operational altitude and speed. Because, employing Western methods, the design and manufacture of an aircraft with the capabilities imputed to the MiG-25 would require an extremely high level of technology, the West feared the Russians had attained such a level. Because modern Western aircraft are designed to perform multiple missions—to intercept, dogfight, bomb—the West assumed that the MiG-25 functioned as a fighter as well as an interceptor.

But Belenko explained and his plane proved that the MiG-25 was not a fighter, not an air superiority aircraft designed to duel with other fighters. Against Western fighters, it would be, as Representative Carr claimed, virtually helpless. But the Russians never intended it to tangle with hostile fighters.

Once the false premises were rectified and the true origin and mission of the MiG-25 understood, then scientific detective work gradually unveiled a picture not so comforting or reassuring.

By 1960 the Russians had seen coming at them over the horizon a fearsome new threat in the B-70, which the United States was planning as the world's fastest and highest flying bomber. To counter the B-70, they had to build rather quickly an interceptor of unprecedented capabilities, one able to achieve Mach 3 at 80,000 feet. The problem was formidable, and the Russians were too poor, materially and technologically, to adopt an American approach in trying to solve it.

They lagged in metallurgy and particularly the exploitation of titanium, which although extremely expensive and hard to work with, is very light, strong, and heat-resistant. And the Americans deemed titanium or some more exotic metal essential to a high-altitude supersonic aircraft. The Russians lagged even more woefully in the technology of transistors, semiconductors, and integrated circuitry, the tininess, lightness, and reliability of which the Americans also considered essential. The only air-to-air missiles the Russians could count on in the foreseeable future would be big, heavy, and short-range.

The Russians lacked the time and resources to develop all the new technology Western designers and engineers doubtless would have thought necessary for the type of interceptor required. So, having no other choice, the Russians elected to make do with what they had. They decided to use, instead of titanium, heavy steel alloy; instead of transistors, vacuum tubes; instead of sophisticated new missiles, those that were available.

This meant that their aircraft would be extraordinarily heavy and could be propelled only by an engine of extraordinary power. But again, they could not afford the many years and billions that design and production of a new engine would demand. So they looked around for something already on hand.

Some years before, the gifted Soviet designer Sergei Tumansky had perfected an engine to power an experimental high-altitude drone or cruise missile. Because of Soviet metallurgical difficulties, he had had to build a big, rugged steel engine, which gulped fuel ravenously. Yet the engine over the years had proved itself highly effective and reliable at altitudes of up to 80,000 feet. Therefore, the Russians decided to create their new interceptor by constructing an airframe around *two* of these powerful Tumansky engines.

They realized that weight and fuel consumption would preclude the aircraft they were conceiving from maneuvering agilely as a fighter and from staying up very long. The plane could be expected only to climb at tremendous speed, like a rocket, fire missiles during one pass at the target, and then land. And that is all the Russians originally expected and designed the MiG-25 to do.

For all their ingenuity in making use of old technology, the Russians recognized they could not avoid innovating some new technology. Old-fashioned vacuum tubes could not accommodate to the sudden and extreme changes in temperature occurring as the plane skyrocketed from the ground to the subfreezing upper air. No pilot, however able, could in the brief time allowed and at the speeds entailed make an intercept without elaborate guidance from the ground. The airborne radar needed to lock onto the target in the final stage of intercept would have to be invulnerable to jamming.

While the Russians urgently concentrated on creating the new interceptor, American aerial strategy and planning suddenly and radically changed. For four years U-2 reconnaissance planes had flown over the Soviet Union with impunity, collecting enormous masses of military, scientific and economic intelligence through photography and electronics, and mapping the country so that it could be bombarded precisely in the event of war. Soviet fighters strained upward, vainly trying to shoot at the U-2 sailing above 60,000 feet, and each time fell back downward in futility. The Russians also had begun to fire surface-to-air missiles, but their guidance systems were not yet effective enough.

On May 1, 1960, the Russians fired a barrage of missiles at a U-2 piloted by Francis Gary Powers. As Belenko was told and as a reliable source affirmed to the United States, some of the missiles hit and destroyed at least one MiG pursuing Powers. But one also hit and downed the U-2. This celebrated incident, coupled with estimates of the future capabilities of surface-to-air missiles, forced a reappraisal of American strategy. Ultimately the Americans concluded that missiles eventually would be so lethal that Soviet air defenses could not be penetrated by high-altitude bombers. Penetration would have to be effected at very low rather than very high altitudes. Therefore, the United States canceled the B-70 bomber.

However, the Russians, whether because of simple bureaucratic inertia, apprehensions that the Americans might reverse themselves, or for occult reasons of their own, proceeded to build the new interceptor. And their decision compounded the mystery of the MiG-25. For to the West, it did not seem logical that they would resort to enormous cost and effort to solve complex technological problems solely to guard against a threat that had been withdrawn.

Years later, in Japan, the more closely and analytically the Americans and Japanese studied the MiG-25, the more clearly they saw how the Russians had overcome the basic and subsidiary problems at comparatively little cost. They, of course, had saved billions in research and development costs by duplicating the dependable old Tumansky engines and relying on steel rather than on titanium. But on those surfaces subject to intense friction and consequent heat, they had affixed strips of titanium. In areas not subject to friction or heat, they had saved more money and some weight by using plain aluminum—something then unthinkable in the West. The rivet heads, it turned out, protruded only in sections where the airflow would not cause any parasitic drag. The rivets, which seemed to reflect crudity of engineering, actually subtracted nothing from aerodynamic performance while they strengthened the plane.

The Russians had brilliantly engineered new vacuum tubes, elevated outmoded technology to a new apex of excellence. They had integrated a superb automatic pilot and a good on-board computer through digital communications to a ground control system that guided the plane to the exact point of intercept. The pilot had merely to take off, turn on the automatic pilot, and await instructions to fire.

Belenko reported that the MiG-25 radar had been described to him as jamproof, and examination confirmed the report. The radar was the most powerful ever installed in any interceptor or fighter, so powerful that it could "burn through" distractive jamming signals transmitted by attacking bombers. The limited range of the radar was irrelevant, for it was needed only to present ground controllers with a magnified image of the target during the last stages of intercept. The search radars that detected and tracked the target at long range were part of the ground control system.

Belenko also stated that despite the disarray, drunkenness, and mutinous atmosphere rife in his regiment, the MiG-25 had been remarkably free of maintenance problems. The reason was that the plane had been designed with the objective of ease and simplicity of maintenance. A mechanic, with modest skills and training, could quickly check critical systems by inserting plugs from test trucks on the runway. All the components most likely to require maintenance were contained in a huge rack situated behind the cockpit. By turning a hydraulic valve, a mechanic could cause the rack to rise out of the plane, and by turning smaller valves, he could cause any separate component to rise out of the box for repair or maintenance.

While the Americans and Japanese methodically denuded the MiG-25 of its secrets, the Russians, posturing, threatening, begging, kept screaming for return of their precious plane. Finally, on November 12—sixty-seven days after its loss—they got it back—in pieces. A procession of eight Japanese tractor-trailer trucks with solemn and ceremonious insult delivered the crates to dockside at the port of Hitachi, where the Soviet freighter *Taigonos* waited with a crew augmented by technicians and KGB officers. The freighter tarried until the Russians inventoried all the parts, making sure that the Dark Forces and their unscrupulous Japanese confederates had kept none. Some 2,000 Japanese police patrolled the dock and many merrily waved as the freighter sailed on November 15.

The Japanese subsequently billed the Soviet Union $40,000 for "damage to ground facilities and transportation charges." The Russians retaliated with a $10 million bill for "unfriendly handling." Neither bill, it is believed, was ever paid.

But the Americans and Japanese gladly would have paid many times $10 million for the aircraft Belenko delivered gratis. General Keegan concluded:

> The MiG-25 had been perceived as an aircraft of awesome potential calling for rapid development on the most urgent national basis of a true air-superiority fighter by the United States.
>
> Belenko has settled, once and for all, the debate about the MiG-25. He has shown us, much to our surprise, that it was not a fighter, that we have nothing to fear from it as a fighter. But at the same time, the aircraft carries with it many sobering lessons for us.
>
> It reflects genius in resources management and magnificent usage of existing resources and primitive ingenuity. By brilliant marriage of ancient and new technology, the Russians developed in a relatively short time and at relatively little cost an aircraft satisfying performance requirements that could not have been achieved in the West except at exorbitant cost.
>
> The fact that the threat the MiG-25 was designed to meet—a high-altitude bomber—never materialized does not mean that their efforts were wasted. The existence of the MiG-25 and our presumptions about it strongly influenced a national political decision not to overfly the Soviet Union with the SR-71 or with reconnaissance drones. Through the MiG-25, the Russians caused us to deny ourselves for years vast amounts of intelligence which could be gathered by no means other than overflights.
>
> The MiG-25 today remains the best tactical reconnaissance aircraft in the world. It can overfly most areas on the periphery of the Soviet bloc with impunity because we have not in most areas deployed the weapons capable of hitting a plane traveling at its speed and altitude. Sure,

the SR-71 would be a better tactical reconnaissance plane if modified for tactical reconnaissance. But to my latest and best knowledge, we have not done that.

In sum, the MiG-25 reminded us that the Russians will go to any ends to meet their military requirements and that despite technological deficiencies they usually do meet them. Were we to apply the lessons apparent in the MiG-25, we could save untold billions of dollars in the development of future weapons systems and develop them far faster than we customarily have.

But Belenko had much more to give than just the MiG-25 and his knowledge of it. Through his eyes the Americans were able to look deeply and searchingly inside the Soviet Air Force and see its strengths and vulnerabilities as never before. In Belenko himself they were able to study the mentality, capacity, and outlook of a Soviet pilot. During the interrogations he increasingly impressed all who worked with him, whether from the military or CIA, by the honesty and the accuracy with which he recounted what he had seen and heard. All that he reported which could be subjected to independent verification proved to be true. And the Americans came to trust him so much that they allowed him to enter and experiment in a combat simulator unknown to most of their own pilots.

It was a space-age creation born of incredible U.S. advances in computer and microcircuitry technology. Three fighter cockpits each were encased in a huge sphere onto whose interior cameras projected startlingly realistic images of sky, earth, horizon, and moving clouds. The images combined with a pressure suit to duplicate the sensations and stresses of flight with such verisimilitude that on occasion experienced pilots had become airsick. Each cockpit could be programmed to emulate the characteristics and performance of a given plane in a given situation.

Accompanied by Gregg, Belenko was told that first he would "fly" a MiG-17. He put on the G—suit, strapped himself into the cockpit, and the sphere closed. Suddenly he was transported not only into the skies but back to the Soviet Union. The stick and controls moved; the whole cockpit seemed to tilt and turn just as the MiG-17s he had long flown in the Caucasus had. Now he saw two other MiG-17s, "flown" by American pilots in the other cockpits, joining him in formation. *I cannot believe it! It is as if I have just taken off from Armavir!*

Successively the simulator was reprogrammed so that Belenko experienced flight in a MiG-21, a MiG-23, and finally his own MiG-25. He had astonished the Americans by the exactitude of Soviet knowledge of the F-4, F-14, F-15, and F-16. Now he realized that they already possessed equal knowledge of all the Soviet aircraft—except the MiG-25. The feel and performance of the MiG-25 they simulated were remarkably close to reality, but they had programmed it as if it could fly at Mach 3.2.

After a day of orienting himself to both American fighters and the MiGs, Belenko "flew" in combat against U.S. pilots and planes. In a MiG-17 and a MiG-21, he shot down F-4s at lower altitudes but was bested by them at higher altitudes. Another exercise pitted Belenko and an American in two MiG-23s, the best Soviet fighter, against an American in the F-15, the best U.S. fighter. At the outset the MiG-23s were given the advantage of higher altitude behind the F-15. At the signal "Go!" they dived toward it at Mach 2.3 to fire their missiles. Suddenly the F-15 disappeared, and Belenko yelled into the microphone to his wingman. "Hey, where is he?" Then a flash in the cockpit signaled that he had been blown up by a missile. Within forty seconds the F-15 had climbed, circled, and destroyed both MiG-23s.

In a MiG-25 Belenko took off against an F-15. Before they reached 50,000 feet, the F-15 shot him down four times, but at about 60,000 feet the MiG-25 accelerated upward and out of range of the F-15.

The combat exercises, each one of which cost $10,000, according to information given Belenko, spanned three days. The results were complex, required lengthy computer analysis, and remain highly classified. But this much can be said: While the F-15 demonstrated its clear superiority over the MiGs, Belenko as a pilot demonstrated himself to be fully the equal of the American fliers against whom he competed.

In time, Belenko visited dozens of U.S. air bases and talked with hundreds of American pilots. As an instructor, a MiG-17, SU-15, and MiG-25 pilot, he had seen dozens of Soviet air bases and spoken with hundreds of Russian fliers. In light of this unique background, he was asked to attempt a comparative appraisal of American and Soviet personnel and aircraft.

He judged that in terms of natural, individual ability the fliers of both nations are about the same. The Russians have tried to adopt American methods of selecting air cadets through psychomotor testing, and a young Russian has an enormous incentive to retain flight proficiency and thereby the enormous privileges which set him apart and far above the citizenry. In contrast with an American pilot, who may begin flight training after studying literature or sociology in a university, Soviet pilots spend years studying aviation and thus have much more theoretical knowledge. They also are generally in better physical condition because they must continuously exercise to pass a rigorous calisthenics test each year. The professional readiness of Soviet pilots probably is deleteriously affected by inordinate amounts of time wasted in political indoctrination, diversion of energies to essentially political duties in overseeing subordinates, and periodic assignments to nonmilitary tasks, such as harvesting or, as at Chuguyevka, road building.

However, Belenko believes that the main reasons the Americans may enjoy an advantage in pilot performance is that they fly more, both during and after training, and they have inherited a wealth of combat experience unavailable to their Soviet counterparts.

There are other Soviet pilots who, presented with the opportunity, would flee with their aircraft, and the Soviet armed forces in general are quite vulnerable to subversion by

Western intelligence services. But were the Soviet Union attacked, most Russian pilots would fight ardently and to the best of their ability to defend not communism necessarily but their Mother Country, to which they are spiritually bound, however ill it may have served them. In his opinion, the large majority of Soviet pilots, if ordered, actually would ram hostile aircraft. With luck they might eject and survive as heroes; without it they would die as heroes, and their families would not suffer. Should they disobey an order to ram, they would be imprisoned and their families would suffer grievously.

Among enlisted personnel supporting flight operations, Belenko considers the American advantage overwhelming. The conditions of life and servitude of Soviet enlisted men are so brutal that they can barely be compelled to perform adequately in peacetime. He questions whether they could be coerced to perform adequately in the chaos and adversity of wartime. In his estimation, American enlisted personnel are incomparably better treated, trained, and motivated and probably would discharge their duties even more zealously and efficiently in wartime than in peacetime.

Finally, Belenko observes that the American air forces benefit from rapid dissemination and adaptation of new technological and tactical data. In the Soviet Union, because of a tradition of secrecy and the effects of the political bureaucracy within the military, communication of new information, much less its exploitation, is slow and difficult.

As for aircraft, Belenko's wide exposure to fighters in the United States has only confirmed what he was told in the Soviet Union. The F-14, F-15, and F-16, along with their missile, radar, and fire-control systems, are appreciably better than their Soviet counterparts, although the United States has not of its own choice developed an interceptor that can match the MiG-25 at the highest altitude.

Before his flight, Belenko was told, accurately, it would seem, that the Soviet Union planned a new version of the MiG-25 with two seats, a look-down radar, more effective missiles, and improved engines that would not accelerate out of control. He doubts, though, that any modifications can over-come the congenital limitations of weight, fuel consumption, range, and maneuverability that doom the MiG-25 to inferior-ity at heights below 60,000 feet.

Some of the most significant revelations from Belenko have been and probably will be kept secret indefinitely, for to disclose them would only assist the Russians in repairing the cracks and crevices he pointed out. And while telling the United States much that it did not know, he was able some-times to show how it had seriously misinterpreted what it did know. "We asked him to look at an elaborate analysis of some-thing our cameras detected by chance when there was an abnormal opening in clouds that normally covered a particu-lar region. Learned men had spent vast amounts of time try-ing to figure out what it was and concluded that it was some-thing quite sinister," an Air Force officer said. "Viktor took one look at it and convincingly explained why what we thought was so ominous was in fact comically innocuous."

Upon completion of the formal debriefings of Belenko, which lasted roughly five months, General Keegan com-mented: "The value of what he gave us, what he showed us is so great that it can never be measured in dollars. The people of the United States and the West owe him an everlasting debt. He grew up in a brutal, bestial society. In the military, he lived, despite his elite status, in a moral junkyard. Yet he came out of it as one of the most outstanding young studs, one of the most honest, courageous, self-reliant young men I have ever known of. I would love to have him as a pilot in the U.S. Air Force or Navy."

Other Americans who came to know Belenko felt much the same way. But his future was far from secure. He had yet to confront the greatest crisis of his life.

CHAPTER
VIII

The
Final
Escape

The CIA and Air Force did their best to steel Belenko against one danger that was foreseeable.

No matter how knowledgeable, perspicacious, intelligent, and helpful an escapee from the Soviet Union may be, there inevitably arrives a time when his special knowledge is exhausted. The initial, intense drama that binds interrogated and interrrogators together personally and intellectually in a common cause sooner or later must end. The Americans who have been daily or frequent companions, who have formed for the Russian a kind of spiritual lifeline in a bewilderingly strange society must disperse and depart for other duties. And the Russian must begin a new life which only he can finally forge.

The KGB habitually warns military officers, Soviet civilians allowed abroad, and its own personnel that should they defect, "The Americans will squeeze you like a lemon, and once they have squeezed you dry, they will throw you into the garbage like a peel." Unless the transition from dependence to independence is accomplished adroitly, the Russian may feel that he is being thrown away. The consequent sense of abandonment, betrayal, aimlessness, and loneliness can cause disabling depression or destructive paranoid behavior.

Throughout the months of interrogation, Gregg, Anna, Peter, and others strove to gird Belenko for the transition by frankly explaining what it eventually would entail, exposing him to differing facets of American society, and giving him practical knowledge. Anna stimulated him to think about making the kind of choices, large and small, which are mostly unnecessary in the Soviet Union. To illustrate, she asked: Do most Soviet citizens have to decide which apartment or house they will rent or buy, where they will shop, which type of clothes to wear, which television station to watch, which newspapers to read, which brands of products they prefer, where they will vacation, which route to take when traveling, in which motel or hotel they will stay, which theater to attend, which make of car they will drive and where they will buy it, which physician will treat them?

No, of course not. In that country you take whatever they will give you, whatever you can find. You don't choose. They choose. Or luck chooses.

The CIA deliberately waited until the end of the interrogations to prepare Belenko financially. He never asked for or about money; he worked and gave sedulously of his own free will. By waiting until all had been given, the CIA tried to connote to him its appreciation that neither he nor all he brought was for sale. Nevertheless, both fairness and U.S. national interests required handsome recompense. The value of Belenko's contributions, as everyone who knew of them agreed, was inestimable, and however indifferent he was to money, he deserved reward. Successfully and healthily integrated as an American, he would remain an asset to the military and intelligence establishment for many years. His success in the United States would tend to invite future defections; his failure, to deter them.

Hence, the CIA told Belenko that the United States felt it owed him a debt. Considering the sacrifices of status and career he had made to give so much to the United States, it would be unfair to ask him to start in a foreign country with nothing. Accordingly the CIA had established an irrevocable trust, to be managed by competent financial experts, that would yield him a generous income for the rest of his life.

With this guaranteed income, Belenko could live anywhere he wished, do virtually anything he wanted without having to earn a living. He could enroll in a university and take a degree in any of the subjects that had engrossed him as an adolescent—medicine, biology, psychology, physics. He could open some kind of shop to exercise his mechanical aptitudes and interests. He could make his way into commercial aviation. Or he could do nothing except fish, hunt, read, and fly his own private plane.

Belenko was grateful for the offer and the way it was made, but it did not overjoy him or resolve any of the issues that most concerned him. Although he came from a society where scarcity obsesses most people with materialism, he was one of the least materialistic of men. He did not have a pair of shoes until he was six, wore the same shirt and trousers for five years as a teenager, and, aside from his uniforms, never owned a suit until the Japanese gave him one. After marriage, he purchased a television, refrigerator and furniture, not for himself but in hope of pleasing and making a home for his bride. He felt no impulse now to compensate or overcompensate for past deprivations; he still aspired to live by the code of Spartacus. He did cherish the Air Force flight suit and the Navy flight jacket; he did want a car because in America it was a necessity and an instrument of freedom. Otherwise, he did not covet material possessions.

The superabundance he saw in the United States intrigued and excited him because of what it signified—a system that had already produced what the Soviet system all his life had promised but was light-years away from delivering. Before attempting to create a place, a purpose, and freedom for himself within the American system, he needed to discover and understand how and why the system worked.

They are not throwing me away like a lemon. They mean to be fair, to be kind to me. But I must find my own way. I must prove I can make my own way. I will accept their offer, and it can be my parachute if I fail. But until I see whether I can survive by myself, I will take only enough money to start.

Partly consciously, partly unconsciously, Belenko determined to explore the United States through Soviet eyes, to assess it according to all he had been taught in the Soviet Union. Though already persuaded that much of what he had been told was false, he thought that the Dark Forces had exposed him only to the best and that he should first examine the worst. The worst in the Soviet Union, outside a concentration camp, was a farm, so he announced that he wished to work for a while on a farm.

Fine, said the CIA. It would try to help him obtain a job as a farmhand. First, though, he must undergo a complete physical examination; then he should spend a month or so in a quiet university environment improving his English and learning more about how to navigate socially on his own.

For the physical, Belenko flew with Gregg to Brooks Air Force Base in San Antonio. Having been looked at by a physician almost every day of his life as a Soviet pilot and thoroughly examined every six months, he considered the venture pointless and boring.

He was shocked when an Air Force dentist informed him that five teeth recessed in his gums would have to be extracted and seven others filled or capped. Remembering the agony of having had a tooth pulled in Rubtsovsk, he argued vehemently that no such necessity could exist; else the many dentists who had inspected his mouth over the years would have recognized it. The dentist displayed X rays, pointed out the troublesome teeth, and projected the decay and infection that would ensue unless they were removed. An anesthetic induced euphoria, then unconsciousness, and Belenko was bothered for only a couple of days of tolerable soreness.

The painlessness of the procedure, the detection of his atrocious dental condition, the thoroughness with which he was examined, and the immaculate hospital impressed him. *Here is a big chance. It's obvious they're good doctors. They*

should know. Probably they're good men and will tell the truth.
Go ahead. Ask them.

No Party defamation of the United States had affected Belenko more than the Soviet descriptions of American medical care. He still believed that medical treatment in the United States was so expensive that unless one was rich or privileged, serious illness or accident meant financial ruin, irreversible impoverishment. The specter of untold numbers of American workers and their families suffering, maybe even dying, because they feared the catastrophic costs of visiting a physician or hospital proved in his mind that at least in one important respect capitalism was inferior to communism, which provided free medical care. He knew, of course, that Soviet medical care often was inadequate and distributed unequally. How else to account for the flourishing medical black market? If one wanted to ensure oneself or a loved one a first-class appendectomy performed under sanitary conditions by a skilled surgeon at night in his office, one made a deal with the doctor. (In 1976 the going rate for a black market appendectomy was 100 rubles.) Still, if one waited and took his chances, medical care was free, just as his dental care had been.

So Belenko put the military doctors through a polite inquisition. Is this a typical American hospital? How much does it cost to stay in a hospital? To pay a doctor? How can a worker afford it? How can someone very old or poor afford it? How much does a doctor earn? A nurse? How long do you have to wait to see a doctor? To get into a hospital?

The physicians enhanced their credibility to Belenko by prefacing their answers with some qualifications. Medical care in the United States *was* expensive and becoming more so. The rising costs, the causes of which were many, concerned everybody. A disadvantaged minority of Americans probably did not receive care that was adequate by American standards, but the reasons often were sociological and cultural rather than medical or economic. And there were exceptions to the best generalizations they could offer. Then they answered his questions, and their answers flabbergasted him.

What! You mean they pay a doctor twice as much as a fighter pilot? You mean you pick your own doctor, and if he makes you wait too long or you don't like the way he treats you, you go to another doctor? That means he has to try to treat all his patients well, or they'll go somewhere else. And you can sue a doctor or the hospital if they do something wrong.

Wait a minute. Nobody ever told me the government pays for the old and the poor. And nobody ever told me about this insurance. Nobody ever said anything about insurance paying most of the bills. They lied. All these years, they lied, and they knew they were lying!

By some artifice, the CIA arranged for Belenko to audit courses temporarily at a medium-sized southern university, and he, together with a young CIA officer, rented an apartment near the campus. Representing himself as a visiting Norwegian eager to learn about the United States, he mingled among students, inquiring about their backgrounds, how they qualified for the university and supported themselves. He reconnoitered the medical school and noted all he would have to do to become a physician. One weekend he went from service station to service station asking for a job as a mechanic, and two stations offered him part-time jobs. He reckoned that he could earn at least $120 a week while attending school, and it would be much easier to work while attending an American university because no time was wasted on political indoctrination.

In this country, unless you are very stupid, you can go to a university of some kind no matter whether you are rich or poor, male or female, black or white, young or old. If I passed the entrance examination, I could do it. I could be a doctor. Even if I did not receive a scholarship, I could borrow money from the government. Even if I could not borrow money, I could earn enough as a mechanic. I would have to work hard at night and on the weekend and in the summer. So what? I could do it without anybody's help.

Someone in the CIA, through a friend, steered him to a family farm more than half a continent away from Washington. Yes, they needed a farmhand, and they would be pleased to take a young Russian and tell nobody he was Russian, provided he was able and willing to work just like anybody else at standard wages. Belenko was drilled in methods of secretly communicating with the CIA, given emergency numbers, and assured that a call day or night would bring instant help. Gregg and Peter also gave him their home numbers and urged him to call whenever he felt like talking. And the CIA emphasized that all the money and support he might need were cached in Washington.

Before he left, Anna gave a party for him, serving deviled eggs with caviar, herring, smoked salmon, borscht, onion and tomato salad, piroshki, Georgian wine, and Russian vodka. She played the guitar and sang Russian folk songs, and some of the Americans, all of whom spoke Russian, joined her. They told Russian jokes and stories and danced as in Russia.

Their efforts, however, affected Belenko differently from the way they had intended. *What is the matter with you? I'm homesick. I miss my rotten country. Idiot! Don't think like that. That is dangerous.*

Belenko arrived by bus at the farm in the late afternoon, and the owner, Fred, his wife, Melissa, and partner, Jake, greeted him on the front porch of the large frame farmhouse painted white with green shutters. Supper, as they called it, was waiting, and after washing, he joined them and their three children around a long oak dining table laden with country food—pickled ham, relish, veal cutlets, corn on the cob, fresh green beans with onions and new potatoes, hot biscuits, iced tea, and peach cobbler with whipped cream. Always, in a new social situation, Belenko watched what the Americans did and tried to emulate them, so when they bowed their heads, he did the same. Fred said a brief prayer, and Belenko did not understand it all; but one sentence touched him: "Bless this home, our family, and he who joins us." He thought far back through the years to the cold, barren day when his father had left him on another farm, the *kolkhoz* in Siberia. The squalid Siberian hut where he had been given milk and bread and the spacious farmhouse with all its largesse were as different as the moon and earth. But the spirit in which he was welcomed at each farm was the same.

Heretofore Belenko had thought that corn on the cob was fed only to livestock, and he tasted it with reservation. *This is good! I wish I could send some to hell for Khrushchev.* All the food was good. His conspicuous enjoyment of it pleased Melissa, and the knowledge he exhibited during talk about farming pleased the men.

He had heard about it; he had read about it; he had glimpsed signs of it from roads and the sky. But Belenko had to experience the efficiency of an American farm to comprehend. His understanding began in the morning as Fred showed him the equipment—a tractor, combine, harvester, machinery for seeding, irrigating, fertilizing, an electronically controlled lighting system that caused hens to lay eggs on schedule, automatic milking devices, two cars, a large pickup truck—and then Belenko saw, of all things, an airplane.

"Why do you have an airplane?"

"Oh, I was in the Air Force; gunner, not a pilot. But I still got the bug, and it's stayed with me. The plane comes in handy. We can get anything we need in a hurry and look over the whole place in fifteen to twenty minutes. Mostly, though, I keep it because for some reason I just like to fly."

"I understand your feelings."

"You ever fly?"

"Yes."

"Good! Would you like to go up with me on Sunday?"

"Very much."

In a few days Belenko deduced that beyond mechanization, there were two other reasons that enabled Fred, his wife, their children, Jake, and one laborer—himself—to work the farm embracing several hundred acres of cultivated land plus pasture and woodland. Fred and Jake knew about every scientific aspect of farming—veterinary medicine, fertilization, use of pesticides, crop rotation, irrigation. For almost twenty years they had kept meteorological records so they could make their own weather forecasts. They could service and repair all the machinery themselves. Along with Melissa, they were accountants and salesmen. And they worked, hard, carefully, enthusiastically, from sunrise to sunset, taking off only Sunday and sometimes Saturday afternoon. *They treat this whole farm as if it were their private plot. Well, of course. That's right. It is.*

On Sunday afternoon they took off in a Beechcraft from a grassy landing strip, climbed about 1,000 feet into cloudless sky, and flew in a rectangle, roughly tracing the farm boundaries. Fred ascended to 8,000 feet, described neighboring farms and their history, and then flew over the two nearest small towns. "Would you like to try the controls?"

Belenko nodded. Having flown a Beechcraft in Virginia, he knew its capabilities and limitations, and he banked easily 180 degrees to the left, then 180 degrees to the right, looking to ensure no other planes were in the vicinity.

"You really are a flier."

"Do you like aerobatics?"

"Okay. Go ahead. But remember, we don't have chutes."

The urge was childish but overpowering. Quickly he looped the plane, started another loop, and at the top flipped over, executing an Immelmann with which he had impressed Nadezhda. He rolled, stalled, spun, did every maneuver the plane could safely withstand. At first, Fred laughed and shouted, like a boy on a roller coaster. Suddenly he fell silent, and seeing him paling, Belenko leveled off. "I am sorry. I am acting like a fool."

"No, that's all right. Take her down."

Fred said nothing during descent, landing, or while they lashed the wings and tail to mooring rings, and Belenko was sure he had angered him.

"I'm afraid you have told me something you didn't mean to. You're the MiG-25 pilot, aren't you?"

You are a fool, Belenko! A snotty-nosed fool!

"Don't worry. I won't tell anyone. We thought we'd found ourselves a real good farmhand. I realize now that you'll be moving on. So I'll say only this. As long as I live, you'll have a home on this farm, and you can come and go as you please."

Fred kept the secret, and Belenko continued to labor as an ordinary farmhand, driving the tractor, plowing, seeding, digging irrigation ditches, feeding cows and pigs, helping build a new barn and maintain the machinery. In return, he received $400 a month, free medical insurance, a cottage with a living room, bedroom, kitchen and bath, free meals with the family or all the food he wanted to cook himself, and use of one of the family cars in the evening and on weekends. These all were perquisites promised at the time he was hired.

Having recognized his identity, Fred additionally allowed Belenko to fly with him on weekends and, if he could be spared from work, on cross-country trips. Studying private and commercial aviation in the United States, Belenko concluded that even were he to start as a penniless farmhand, he eventually could become a ranking airline pilot. In Russian he drafted a program entitled "How to Be 747 Pilot—My Plan."

He calculated that in three years he could easily save from his wages $12,000 which would more than pay for the 40 hours of flight time necessary for a private license and the additional 160 hours requisite to a commercial license. Once licensed, he would take any job as a commercial pilot, gain the reputation of a skilled, reliable flier, and prepare himself for airline examinations. Then he would work his way upward from copilot on small jets to the 747.

It will take maybe twenty years. But it can be done. Also, private pilots here are very friendly. They will let you fly with them for nothing. So I could get a lot of free flight time.

At harvesttime they employed temporary workers, combines came from nearby farms, and in three days 400 acres of tall green corn were transformed into what looked like a pretty meadow. *That was a miracle. No, it was not. Anybody could do it — if he had the machines, and the machines worked, and he knew how and was free to do it.*

The night harvesting ended, they sat on the front porch and drank cold hard cider. It reminded Belenko of the homemade wine the farmers had given the air cadets and students summoned into the orchards outside Armavir. The mechanism of the mind which often and mercifully deadens memories of the bad blocked out the sight of tens of thousands of apples rotting, of the system that made every harvest a national crisis.

That was a good time. The girls were pretty, the fruit sweet, the farmers friendly. We had fun. I wish I could see Armavir just for one day, hear nothing but Russian just for a day.

In his sleep a terrible vision visited him. Vorontsov was smiling, beckoning, calling, and pulling him from the State Department conference room with an invisible chain wrapped around his waist. "It is time, Viktor Ivanovich. You are coming home. Come with me, Viktor Ivanovich." He awakened shouting, *"Nyet, nyet!"*

That was a ridiculous dream. You drank too much of that cider. Take some aspirin, and go to sleep.

Reflecting on the nightmare in the morning and vaguely sensing its portent, Belenko undertook to exorcise the causes by assaying his experiences in rural America. *You came out here looking for the worst, and what did you find? These farmers, they live better than almost anybody in Moscow or Leningrad. I'm not even sure that Politburo members can buy in Moscow everything you can buy out here in Sticksville. Why, a common laborer on this farm is better off than a Soviet fighter pilot. And you don't have to put up with all that shit, from the first day of school until the last day you breathe. These farmers, they don't listen to anything they don't want to. They just show the government or anybody else the big finger. They are not afraid. They are free people. They say all their guns are for hunting. But they would shoot anybody who tried to deport them or take away their freedom.*

And the way they do things works. Look at the harvest! Did they bring in the Air Force and the Army and students and workers from two hundred fifty kilometers away and screw around for weeks and let a third of the crop rot because the machinery broke down and nobody knew or cared what he was doing?

Lied! It's worse than lying. The Party turned the truth upside down. It's the kolkhozniks *who are the serfs. No wonder a farmer here produces ten times as much as a* kolkhoznik! *No wonder they have to buy from the Americans! Don't forget that. Don't forget what you've seen with your own eyes, here and there.*

After this analysis and introspection Belenko concluded there was no more to learn on the farm, and he had already recognized an insuperable defect in his plan to obtain pilot's licenses while working on the farm. To fly commercially or even alone and to investigate the United States as thoroughly as he wished, he would have to improve his mastery of English markedly. So when the CIA summoned him to Washington to confer about some sensitive new matters, he decided to leave permanently and immerse himself wholly in language study.

Fred flew Belenko to the airport of a city some 150 miles distant. "Remember, you always have a home."

From a list compiled by Peter, Belenko chose a commercial institute specializing in teaching foreigners seeking high proficiency in English. Peter suggested that before departing, he ought to buy a car, gave him some automotive magazines, and took him to several dealers. *You can buy a car in this country as easily as a loaf of bread! Everybody wants to sell me a car! They don't care whether I can pay for it now or not. Just give them a few hundred dollars, and they give you a car. How can they trust people like that?*

Driving alone in his new medium-sized sedan, Belenko experienced both another form of freedom and bewilderment as he headed into the South on multilane interstate highways. *It's just as Father Peter and Anna said. You don't have to ask anybody permission to go anywhere. With a car and a map, you can drive anywhere day or night, and always you can find fuel and food. How can they afford to let everybody just get up and go anywhere he pleases whenever he wants? What keeps order in this country?*

Study at the institute was intellectual fun. Most of the students, drawn from all parts of the Middle East, Asia, and South America, were as serious as the demanding instructors who proceeded on the thesis that the secret of mastering a foreign language is sheer hard work. The students had to listen, drill, recite, and converse eight hours daily, take exams after regular classes, and do homework at night. As his command of English grew under this regimen so did his power to indulge his fondness of reading. Periodically he brought home from the public library armloads of books, particularly the works of George Orwell, Arthur Koestler, and Milovan Djilas, which refined his understanding and hardened his hatred of Soviet communism.

But the more he delved into daily American life, the further the fundamental understanding he sought seemed to recede from his reach. Looking for the cheapest apartment available, he rented one in what he was told was a working-class neighborhood. Although not as commodious as that in Virginia, the apartment was by the standards he knew luxurious, and everything functioned: the air conditioning, stove, plumbing, garbage disposal. Talking and sometimes drinking beer with the neighbors, he learned that they indeed were what he would term workers, and not only could they afford to rent apartments like his for $200 monthly, but some actually planned to buy their own houses. From them he also began to learn about labor unions, collective bargaining, and strikes, all of which utterly mystified him.

The Party described American labor unions as subterfuges by which the Dark Forces more handily controlled and manipulated workers. The few strikes reported were represented as impulses of revolution, which, of course, the police lackeys of the Dark Forces would quickly crush, rather than as a form of normal labor relations. When Belenko saw his first picket line, he saw another great lie.

They turned the truth upside down again! What they said American labor unions are is just what Soviet labor unions are. Why, these workers and their unions can shut down a whole factory by just walking out and demonstrating. What would have happened if we had done that at the tank factory? But how can you allow that? How can you allow workers to stop production if they don't think they're paid enough? That doesn't make any sense. It's chaos.

Although he got along amicably with his fellow students, Belenko had no close friends among them because he preferred to associate outside the institute with Americans who could educate him about the United States. There was one student, however, whom he delighted in seeing. Maria was an exquisite young woman, an arresting figure in yellow or brightly printed dresses or white lace blouses, a classic Latin beauty with flowing black hair, dark eyes, full lips, and a soft olive complexion. Beyond the beauty he could see, Belenko sensed in her presence the grace and confidence of a lady whose inner security enabled her to laugh, tease, and be at ease with anyone. She brightened his thoughts as a fresh flower might, and sometimes he wondered if the librarian who had benefited him when he was a boy in Siberia might not many decades before have been like her.

In one of the group discussions a young Iranian, who sported a $20,000 Mercedes, orated about the "plastic society" and materialism of the United States, citing Coca-Cola, fast-food chains, neon signs, and trash along the highways as examples. As if challenged to a fight, Belenko instinctively stood up. "Which society led man into the nuclear age? Which society led man into space and the moon? If we were in your country, what would happen to us if we openly said what we thought was bad about it? If this society is so terrible, why have we all come from our own countries to learn here? Why here instead of some other society?"

As he was walking toward his car after class, Maria called to him to wait for her. "I agree with what you said, and I am proud of you for saying it." They began discussing their reactions to the United States, comments from one excited comments from the other, and they stood, each holding three or four books, talking for nearly an hour before Belenko proposed dinner.

Maria ordered rum and Coca-Cola, which Belenko thought a comical concoction. "No, it is not. If that Iranian knew you are supposed to put rum in Coca-Cola, he would not denounce it."

Answering his questions, Maria told him of her background. Her parents owned a plantation in South America, but she had attended a university and resolved to do something worthwhile. The only practical choices that seemed to be available to her as a woman were teaching or nursing, so she had chosen to be a teacher in rural areas, where teachers were most needed. There she had become interested in helping the mentally handicapped and retarded children for whom no organized, scientific programs were offered. Because so much of the research concerning birth defects and retardation was conducted in the United States, she desired to broaden her knowledge of English, and when her parents, anxious to get her out of the countryside, offered her a trip to the United States, she decided to study at the institute.

According to the custom of her class and culture, her parents virtually had arranged for her to marry the scion of a neighboring plantation family. Although she scarcely knew the man and had not yet consented, her sense of duty and devotion to her aging parents made refusal difficult.

She found the United States largely a classless society; at least she had been able to meet and relate to people irrespective of their social origins or economic status. In her opinion, the opportunities in America were limitless, and personally she would have liked to stay. But she knew that all her life she would feel guilty if she did not return to her own land and do whatever she could to help her people.

He asked her to dance, and on the small floor she gently

pulled him close to her. "You dance as if you were a prize fighter and I your opponent. Hold me lightly. Or tightly, if you want."

He drove her home and bade her good-night with a handshake. Lying awake, he visualized her dancing and felt her again in his arms. *She is as beautiful inside as she is outside. She knows something about life, what is real, what is useless. We think the same. I speak only a few words, and she understands all I mean to say. She is all I ever wanted. But she is going back to her country in a couple of months. I cannot follow her. I cannot ask her to give up her country and stay with me. I do not know what will happen to me. I cannot even tell her who I really am. I care too much for her. I must not see her anymore. To go further will only hurt us both.*

Aside from exchanging greetings at the institute, he did not talk with her again until the night of a party at the home of an instructor. Having asked each student to prepare a dish typifying the cuisine of his or her country, the instructor put Maria and Belenko in charge of the kitchen, perhaps because they, along with a young French businessman, were the quickest pupils. The kitchen was hot and crowded, and they were kept busy washing pots, pans, and dishes, but they performed these pedestrian chores as a natural team, each eager to help the other. She reached up with a damp towel and wiped perspiration from his forehead. Once their eyes met, and neither could deny nor disguise the magic between them. *Anything with her is joy.*

The class collected money to buy the instructor a gift in appreciation of the party and appointed Maria and Belenko to pick out the present. After they went shopping on a Saturday morning, his desire to be with her longer prevailed over his judgment, and he invited her to lunch. It was so easy to talk with her that he found himself expressing thoughts he had never articulated to anyone. "I believe there is a higher purpose in life than just surviving, just having all the possessions and money you need. I don't know what the purpose is. But I think each person has to be free to the purpose."

"Do you believe in God?"

"I don't know. I think there must be something higher than man. But I don't understand what it is. Do you?"

"I want to. All my life I have gone to church. Sometimes the music and quiet are very beautiful to me, and I feel as you, that there is something higher. Then I see things that the church does, and I am not sure. It is said in church that God is love. Maybe that is the purpose. To love someone and be loved by someone."

The drift seemed dangerous to Belenko, and he suggested they go.

"Only if you will make me a promise."

"What is that?"

"The week from tomorrow I am invited to the home of some friends of my parents. They live about forty miles away. Promise that you will take me."

Belenko, blond, fair, blue-eyed, with the athletic bearing of an officer, and Maria, her dark beauty adorned in lace and long white skirt, formed a striking couple, and the Spanish family welcomed them graciously to their American replica of a small hacienda. The host and hostess were especially interested in meeting a Russian. In accordance with the story prepared by the CIA for his use at the institute, he explained that he had fled while serving as a junior official on a Soviet trade mission to Scandinavia. His fresh perspectives of the Soviet Union, which conformed to the antipathies of the host, made him all the more popular.

Belenko had thought they were to stay all day, but after a lavish luncheon Maria eloquently thanked the family, in English for his benefit, and announced that they must depart to prepare for examinations the next day; that was not true.

"Why did you do that?"

"I wanted to be with you."

"We won't be able to be with each other much more. You leave next week, don't you?"

"That is why I want to be with you now. May I tell you something?"

"Of course."

"You will not make fun of me?"

"Certainly not."

"I love you."

"But why?"

"It is the way I feel. I have never had such a feeling. When I am with you or see you or think of you, I am happy. I do not know where you have been or who you were. But I know you, Viktor."

"We will only hurt each other. After a few more days we can never see each other again."

"Do you like me?"

"I love you."

On a Friday afternoon he drove her across the state to the airport from which she would fly out of his life in the morning. Throughout their discussions they spoke rationally, responsibly, bravely.

They realized that genuine love does not spring up suddenly, spontaneously, magically, that it evolves gradually through shared experiences, interests, adversities. They recognized that they had known each other far too briefly to be sure that they were not just ephemerally and romantically attracted. And their backgrounds, their cultures were so different that these differences were bound to assert themselves in the future, no matter how harmoniously they got along now. Of course, Maria could not repudiate her obligations to her parents, her customs, her people and country. She never could be at ease with her conscience or happy outside her own country. No (for reasons he could not explain), he could not live in South America. Should they keep in touch? No, that would only torment them both. Why pursue what never can be? They should be grateful for the lovely friendship they had shared.

After Belenko carried her luggage into the airport motel room where she would sleep until the morning flight, the front collapsed. She sobbed hopelessly, forlornly, as if all life were ending. "Oh, Viktor, spend the night with me."

By dawn he knew that in her and their love he had found a fulfilling purpose of life. *What can I do? I must do what is best for her. She will have a good life without me. I cannot take her away from her family, her people. What can I give to her? I'd better go while I can.*

He dressed quickly, quietly, as he had on the last morning in Chuguyevka. "Darling Maria, it is best if I just go now. Wherever you are, I love you."

Through the closed door, he heard her crying hysterically. *"Sólo tú! Siempre, sólo tú!"*

Shock anesthetized him for a while. Then, on the third or fourth day, the pain struck: ceaseless, incapacitating pain. *You found the greatest beauty and purpose life can hold. And you threw it away. And you can never find it again. You will never see her again.*

At the institute he ceased to function; he could not concentrate or learn. The instructors concluded that the intensity of study had made him stale and that he had reached a plateau which temporarily bogs down the best of language students, and they recommended he take a couple of months off. If he could afford it, they suggested, he should tramp around the country, practicing English.

Wearing his Navy flight jacket, he drove recklessly toward Washington, receiving three speeding tickets on the way, and pulled up, unannounced, at Peter's house. That house, he previously had noted, because of the necessities enforced by eight children, always was run with the same precision as life on an aircraft carrier.

"Father Peter, I have a plan. You send me back to Soviet Union as agent. Drop me in the Far East; I will show you just where to go through the radar. You think it is so difficult to spy in that country. But I know that country, and I can do it so easily. What you Americans never have understood is that you can buy anything in that country, very cheaply too.

"A judge, only two hundred rubles. Plant manager, five hundred. Militiaman, fifty. What we really want we don't have to buy. I can get you a MiG-23 and a Backfire [a Soviet bomber] for nothing. My friends will fly them wherever I say.

"I know that place; I feel it the way nobody who is not Russian can. I can smell; I can move in it. You give me the documents and a little radio the size of my hand—I know from the Air Force you have them; the ones that squeeze and squirt transmissions into seconds—and we can talk every day. Let's go! Let's fight! Let's show them the big finger!"

"Are you all right?"

"What do you mean, all right?"

"The idea is preposterous. Even if it weren't, you're smart enough to know you're much more valuable here than you could ever be there. It seems to me you are under some emotional duress. I'm your friend. What's the trouble?"

The code of Spartacus, which bound a man to solve his own problems, to rely on himself, to whimper to no one for help, clashed with his honesty, and uncharacteristically he compromised. He accurately reported the institute's advice that he travel for a while, briefly mentioned his relationship with Maria, and confessed to some sadness at her loss.

"Do you love this girl?"

"Yes, I do."

"Do you want us to find her for you?"

"No. It makes no sense. I do not belong in her life."

"Would you like one of us to go along on your trip?"

"I must go by myself."

"All right, but I want the doctors to see you." Physicians, to whom he confided nothing of his psychological trauma, pronounced him totally fit, and he drove off to explore, discover, forget, and mend by himself.

He first wanted to tour the small towns, backwashes, and heartland cities because they were the milieu he knew best in the Soviet Union. Conditioned to husband every kopeck, he searched out the cheapest lodging and cafés, although large, unspent sums and the interest on them were piling up monthly for him in Washington. He learned that in almost every small town there is a motel or hotel cheaper than the

Holiday or Ramada inns, which he deemed luxurious hostelries. These lesser-known family establishments invariably were clean, and you could get an inexpensive meal providing all the protein you wanted.

In a little Appalachian town he took a room in such a motel and asked the woman at the desk where he could obtain ice. "If'n you wahnt ais, go dowen the hall and torn laift."

"I don't want ass. I want ice."

"Jes go lik'n I saed."

After a drink he returned to the desk and inquired if the town had a hospital. "Ain't no cause to go to the hospital. Doc will come righ heah."

"I'm not sick. I just want to see the hospital."

Probably persuaded she was dealing with an authentic nut, the woman gave directions, to be rid of him, and at the hospital an intern, upon hearing that he was a visiting Norwegian, volunteered to show him around. It was a small hospital with only thirty rooms, but they were even nicer than those at the Air Force hospital in San Antonio, and the intern's answers were consistent with explanations of American medicine he had received in Texas.

"What are you building out there?" The intern described the functions of a mental health clinic, which in this case would include treatment of mentally handicapped children. Belenko saw a dirty, feebleminded boy of twelve or thirteen wandering the muddy streets of Chuguyevka, a child destined to live his blurred, uncomprehending life unhelped, the butt of jokes and pranks, the village idiot whose purpose was to amuse by his idiocy and make his superiors glad of their superiority. He saw her, too.

Only you. Always, only you, Viktor. Oh, Maria, where are you?

On the road again, he stopped and talked casually with strangers in small Kentucky and Missouri towns; some revelations congealed in his thoughts. *Many Americans would rather live in small towns or the country. Why? Because in many ways life is easier and better for them. They don't have to go to the city to buy food and clothes. The government doesn't allocate supplies first to some cities, second to others, third to the small towns, and fourth to the sticks.*

And where are all the criminals? Where are the fences? Why, in Rubtsovsk or Omsk or Salsk, if you didn't have high fences around houses like the ones everyone lives in here, and dogs, too, the criminals would loot everything! The Americans, they complain about crime. They don't know what crime really is. Let someone strip the clothes and underwear off their wives or daughters at knifepoint in broad daylight on a street corner just so they can sell those clothes and underwear, and they will begin to understand crime.

In Kansas City, Belenko visited the farmers' market, the greatest, most dazzling assemblage of food and produce he had ever seen, and all so cheap. No residual doubts or reservations could withstand the sight. Before his eyes stretched the final, conclusive proof.

No, this system works. They can produce enough food for ten countries, for twenty countries if they want. If anybody goes hungry in this country, he's just stupid.

From the market he wandered into a seedy section of the inner city and there at last found it—something just like in the Soviet Union: a stinking, dark bar crowded with bleary-eyed, unshaved, unkempt drunks growing drunker on beer and cheap rye whiskey. Ah, he knew them well; he had seen them all his life. What he had seen in America usually seemed initially like a mirage; this was real, and he was quite at home.

Sipping a beer, he questioned the bartender. Where do these men work? How do they get off from their jobs in the day? How much do they earn? The bartender, after a fashion, explained the unemployment compensation, welfare, and food stamp programs.

What! You mean in this country you don't have to work even if there is a job for you! You mean the government pays you and gives you food so you can be a deadbeat and sit around and drink all day! Why, the Americans have done it! They have built True Communism! It's just like 1980!

Walking from the bar along a deserted street at dusk, Belenko recognized trouble ahead. Two thugs were eyeing him, wavering in their judgment as to whether they could take him. He knew them well, too. Rather than wait for them, he ran at them and belligerently demanded directions to his motel, which in their surprise they gave.

"How about giving us a quarter?" one said.

"My pockets are full of quarters. But not one quarter I have says deadbeat on it." They turned away, maybe sensing they were confronted by someone who hungered to hit them.

The pristine mountains and cool, pure air of Colorado made him think of parts of the Caucasus, and an indoor skating rink recalled good times skating in Rubtsovsk and Omsk, and he saw Nadezhda gliding toward him, waving. *I would like to see her and my friends just for a day. Skate in the park; go back to the forests; stop by the factory.*

Las Vegas, in consequence of Party conjurations, always had been the supreme symbol of the iniquities and depravities of capitalism, surpassing even the famous decadence of Hollywood. He fully expected to see couples copulating and gangsters shooting it out on the streets, while the bloated rich played cards amid sniffs of cocaine in opulently upholstered and cushioned casinos. So what he saw disappointed, then surprised, then beguiled, and ultimately entranced.

He marveled that a city so clean, neat, and spacious could rise in the midst of desert. His motel in the center of the city was inexpensive; but the rooms were elegant in size and appointments, and the swimming pool was splendid. The shows at the casinos were excellent, yet also inexpensive, as were the drinks.

I will just drink this cheap whiskey and watch all the people. Look at them. They are all kinds of people, and they are enjoying themselves. It's like a carnival, not a brothel. Of course, they are foolish to gamble. The chances are they will lose their money. But it's their choice. If that's the way they want to have a good time, it's their business. They lied about this city. They lied about everything.

In the awesome grandeur of Wyoming, Montana, and Washington and the national parks, he saw more lies, for the Party said greedy capitalism had raped, robbed, and emaciated all the land. He stayed a night in a logging town set in a valley by a clear river surrounded by mountains. The climate and the expanses were like Siberia, and he longed for Siberia.

About forty miles outside San Francisco, he started noticing signs advertising all sorts of lodging, restaurants, and nightclubs in the city. *That's right. There are no signs outside Rubtsovsk or Omsk or Moscow because there are no places to stay or eat. You stay in the railway station if there's room. Sure, we have signs. They tell how great the Party is, how much the Party is achieving. No signs tell you where to buy sausage.*

He stayed in another downtown motel owned by immigrants from India. His room was clean, cheap, and had a big color television. At his request a taxi driver dropped him off in the "worst area" of downtown San Francisco. It was a cesspool of garish nightclubs, pornographic shops, prostitutes, homosexuals, transvestites, junkies, pimps, filthy, unhealthy-looking dropouts, and rebels against society. He ate in a hole in the wall and felt as if he were in a human zoo, yet the fried fish, fried potatoes, and coleslaw, for which he paid $1.50, were good.

Two prostitutes, one black, one white, tried to lure him into a brothel. "For thirty dollars, we'll give you a real good time."

"What do you mean?"

"Don't be stupid. You know. For thirty dollars you can have both of us."

Here the Party was right. The dregs accumulated here were to him as disgusting as anything the Party ever claimed, and such human waste, insofar as it was visible, would be flushed out of Soviet society.

MiG PILOT

As it was early when he went back to his room, he switched on the television and turned the knob from channel to channel until he saw something very familiar. *How wonderful!* In progress on the screen was a superb public television performance of *Anna Karenina*.

There were so many choices. Before, the discovery and contemplation of them had invigorated and stimulated, as did the contemplation of a daring and original move in chess. Now he didn't care. All visions of what could be were clouded, dulled, marred by yearning for what might have been with her.

At a roadside café near Odessa, Texas, a Latin girl served him. She was not so pretty as Maria, but she smiled and carried herself like Maria. He bolted his meal and raced the breadth of Texas in fewer than twenty-four hours and sped foolishly, suicidally toward the institute.

Everywhere they had been together he revisited. He drove to the hacienda and en route back pulled off the road and stopped about where she had spoken to him. And now a delirium of irrationality afflicted him. It was illogical, senseless, but in its effects on him, it was as real as a typhoid delirium. He wanted to flee from himself, from her, from America, the extravagant successes of which made it seem now like an alien planet where he never could be a normal inhabitant.

Primordial impulses seized and held and pushed him, and he could not resist them. He wanted to feel the mud of the streets, smell the stink in which he had grown up, be among the desolate, cold huts, hear Russian, be in the land of his birth, his people, his ancestors. He was hearing and being drawn by not only the call of the Mother Country, but the Call of the Wild.

Did they not say all I have to do is telephone and in twenty-four hours I will be in Moscow? Did not Brezhnev himself promise they would not punish me? Can I not fight for my people better by being among them? Is not my duty to be with my people as Maria is with hers? I will do it. I will go home.

He left his flight jacket, his flight suit, and everything else in the apartment and started north toward Washington—and the Soviet Embassy.

Great stakes rode with him. His voluntary return would prove to millions upon millions within and without the Soviet Union that the Party was right, that Soviet society was superior to American society, that it was the beacon lighting the way to the future of man. A New Communist Man who had seen and judged, who had been captured and escaped would attest dramatically and convincingly to these truths before all the world.

Crossing the North Carolina border into Virginia, he still was pointed toward the Embassy. But as in all other crises, he tried to be Spartacus, to summon forth the best within himself, to think logically. *Why did you leave? Has anything that made you leave changed? Are there purposes in life higher than yourself? Where could you hurt that system most? What could you do back there even if they didn't punish you? Do you really think they would just say, "Welcome home, Comrade!" Who has lied to you? The Americans or the Party? Would Spartacus surrender?*

About 2:00 A.M. north of Richmond, the fever broke, and Belenko first knew it when his hands began to shake on the steering wheel. He was so physically weak that he had to rest, and he pulled in at a truck stop.

An elderly waitress with faded blond hair and a face worn by many years gave him coffee and studied him. "Honey, you been smoking?"

"What?"

"If you're on pot, you ought to let it wear off before you drive anymore. How about some breakfast?"

"Just leave me alone."

"No, honey, I'm going to get you some breakfast. You need something to eat. It's on the house."

Around 4:00 A.M. he leaned on the doorbell at Peter's house, ringing it continuously until Peter, in pajamas, opened the door. Trained to be most poised in the presence of danger, Peter was calm. "I see you're in trouble. Come in."

Slowly, with shame, Belenko told him, taking almost two hours.

"Viktor, I wish you had called me. But I can't criticize you. This is not uncommon. I should have recognized the signs when you were here last month. Now it's over; you are immunized. It would have been a great tragedy, most of all for you. Someday you will see that because you are the way you are and because there is freedom here, the United States is more your homeland than the Soviet Union ever could be."

"I must go tell Gregg."

"Don't worry about that. Get some sleep. We'll let him know."

"No. I must do it myself."

Harassed by early calls from his Pentagon office, behind schedule, and half-dressed, Gregg was irritated by the unexpected appearance of Belenko.

"I have to talk to you."

"Make it quick; I'm late."

After Belenko had spoken for a couple of minutes or so, Gregg picked up the phone and dialed his office. "I won't be in this morning. Call me here if you need me." He listened without comment or interruption until Belenko concluded his recitation of the crisis he had just survived.

"Viktor, I think you're finally free. Let's take the day off and go fly."

As Belenko climbed up over the Potomac estuary and soared above the Chesapeake Bay, he felt, he knew Gregg was right.

Index